FISHING
THE EUROPEAN COAST

FISHING
THE EUROPEAN COAST

MIKE SMYLIE

For Ana

Front cover photograph: A French sinagot sailing off Douarnenez, Brittany, 2008.
Rear cover photograph: Cornish lugger *Snowdrop* sailing off Douarnenez, Brittany, 2008.

Frontispiece: Krabbenkutters (shrimp boats) from the small harbour of Fedderwardersiel (reg FED), close to the estuary of the River Weser, on Germany's North Sea coast.

First published 2009

The History Press
The Mill, Brimscombe Port
Stroud, Gloucestershire, GL5 2QG
www.thehistorypress.co.uk

© Mike Smylie, 2009

The right of Mike Smylie to be identified as the Author
of this work has been asserted in accordance with the
Copyrights, Designs and Patents Act 1988.

British Library Cataloguing in Publication Data.
A catalogue record for this book is available from the British Library.

ISBN 978 0 7524 4628 8

Typesetting and origination by The History Press
Printed in Great Britain

CONTENTS

ACKNOWLEDGEMENTS

Over the years many people have helped me in my quest in discovering and learning about fishing craft. In no particular order I wish to thank the following people: Mike Craine, Darina Tully, Joe Teesdale, Cormac Levis, Nigel Towse, Jim Devine, Robert Prescott, Donal McPholin, John Bushell, Steve Perham, Hans-Christian Rieck, Hermann Ostermann, Reiner & Petra Schlimme, Edgar Readman, Tom Smith, Simon & Ann Cooper, Petros Kounouklas, Peter Faulkner, Robert Simper, Thedo Fruitof, Joseph Muscat, Kostas Damianidis, Angus Martin, Billy Stevenson, Bill Wakeham, Alan Abbot, John McWilliams, Mary Norton, Cas and Kirsten Trouwborst, Vicco Meyer, and Daniel Bosser. The following institutions have also been very helpful: the Scottish Fisheries Museum, the Fiskeri–og Sofartsmuseet, Esbjerg, Denmark, the National Visserijmuseum of Oostduinkerke, Belgium, the Dutch National Fisheries Museum, Vlaardingen, the Brighton Fisheries Museum, the Maritime Museum of Cesanatico and the Barcelona Maritime Museum.

All photographs and drawings are by the author unless stated.

ONE

INTRODUCTION

At a guess I've been drawing fishing boats since those long-ago school days although, due to a multitude of moves, none of those original sketches remain. Training as a naval architect in the 1970s gave me even more insight into the subtleties of their design and an everlasting appreciation of both their work and appearance. Thus in the mid-1990s, with the formation of the 40+ Fishing Boat Association by Michael Craine and myself to lobby government over the enforced scrapping of decommissioned boats, and the publication of the first editions of our newsletter *Fishing Boats*, came the need to illustrate the newsletter with pen and ink drawings as we had no funds to reproduce photographs at that early stage. From that time onwards I retained most of the drawings I had prepared, and continued making them for various articles. This, then, is a pretty wide selection from the pile I have in my box file. In choosing those included I've tried to create a good cross-section from Europe's coastline, drawings made from forays into some 80 per cent of the countries in the Continent with a sea-fishing tradition.

No one knows when the first fishing boat set out to sea, although river fishing by boat was quite likely the earlier. Mosaics from the Mediterranean show vessels encircling shoals dating from the first century although Egyptian tomb reliefs dated to 6000BC show nets being set. In Britain we also know that Mesolithic man was moving about by boat, again in about 6000BC. These people, primarily wanderers, were also hunter gatherers. Jesus, we are told, sailed aboard fishing boats on the Sea of Galilee around the early years of the first century AD, whilst Caesar noted that wooden boats were in use in Britain sometime after the Roman invasion. Coracles were also noted to have been in use and, as such, probably remain the oldest single type of craft in use, developed from earlier log boats. In Britain it is primarily Wales that is renowned for her coracles, although they were in use

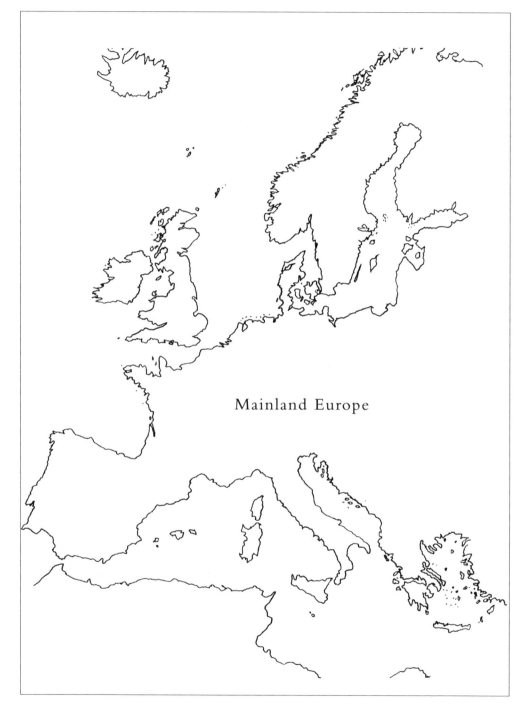

Mainland Europe

MAP OF EUROPEAN COASTLINE

in Ireland, Scotland and England as well as many other parts of the world; India, Iraq and Vietnam coming first to mind. Irish and Scottish currachs were most likely in use for deeper water work at the same time.

However, in these pages, it is really only the last two centuries that concern us. Although the roots of some of the vessels may go back many generations, in the main those in these pages are still in existence in some form or other, even if not for their original intended use. Many have been resurrected by enthusiasts from muddy graves whilst others have continued in service throughout their life. A very few have been reconstructed from drawings and first-hand knowledge of lost vessels. Most of those in the penultimate chapter are still working today. As I said, I've tried to give a good cross-section, although some personal preference has been allowed to dictate the final content because space excludes the complete picture of European fishing boats. That will have to wait a few years more.

Finally, before readers launch into the main body of the book, please let me stress that the order of the boats is purely random. However, by complete chance (or subconscious choice maybe), one of my favourite craft comes first!

TWO

OPEN BOATS
OFF THE BEACH

INTRODUCTION

Common sense tells us that boats working off beaches and riverbanks were the first to be utilised by the developing human race in their desire to spread their wings. Whether these were used to cross rivers and larger stretches of open water, or whether to fish, is unclear although I tend to lean towards the former assumption, the hypothesis being that man had to cross seas to reach the other side simply to develop any pretence of a coastal settlement. The occurrence of fishing by any other means than from the shore prior to this would seem unlikely.

All the boats in this chapter work directly off either beaches or riverbanks, some fishing out into the deep ocean such as the *meia-lua* whilst others worked in the relative quiet of rivers, lagoons and amongst sheltered archipelagos. They represent a broad cross-section of open boats, some being canoe-types whilst others adhere to the generally accepted form of built-up hull. The roots of boatbuilding lie in the log, bark and skin boats and rafts, the log boats themselves developing into plank-on logs in which the log is used as the base of the boat and planks are added along its upper edge to form a larger buoyancy. Such sewn boats are still used extensively in parts of the world, those of India and nearby Sri Lanka being the only ones I've personally considered in any great detail. The log catamarans of southern India represent the basic form of the raft where three or more logs are tied together to create a stable floating platform, and the reed boats of Sardinia are another example of another basic raft. As for the skin boats, the currachs and coracles are perhaps the best examples, the latter being described below.

It is perhaps debatable as to what constitutes an open boat and it will be noted that some of the vessels here, most notably the canoes from the Mesolongi lagoon in Greece, are indeed decked over to a degree. However, I include them in this category for they are by no means sea-going craft. Furthermore, the vessels shown are modern versions of the traditional form and these early vessels operated wholly by oar would have been completely undecked. Meanwhile the argument will rage as to whether a vessel with a very short foredeck with nothing but a tiny storage space below can be termed 'open'. Personally I don't care, in the same way as I don't like to get involved in the replica question for whether a vessel has been totally rebuilt or is considered as a new boat does not concern me. Terminology can be another area of contention. Although academics might discuss in detail the exact term for a particular vessel, those that used the vessel in their working life didn't bother with such trifles. To them their boat was simply that – a boat. However, in terms of ethnology, it is often necessary to be more exacting in describing and giving a name to a particular type. In the vernacular zone this is perhaps more important because of the wide diversity of craft employed in the variety of maritime occupations such as the coastal trade, fishing, pilotage, salvage, life-saving and many more. Often, too, it is difficult to specify borders between each area because of the cross-flow of influences from area to area. This is especially so for the smaller craft for, as designs developed, these borders became much fewer and far between. In the case of fishing boats, this is easy to understand when one considers today's larger trawlers that appear almost identical wherever they work. As the fleets shrank, so did the numbers of builders, so that European fishing boats from any country are as likely to have been built anywhere from Norway to Italy.

One final note – although examples of these boats are easily found today, most do not work. Those few that do are drastically altered to suit modern technology. However, that they have withstood the test of time is surely evidence of the legacy they will one day leave. Let's hope, though, that that day is still long off.

PORTUGUESE *MEIA-LUA*

This has to be one of the most spectacular fishing boats in use on Europe's coastline. One of the best known of Portuguese craft is the open *saveiro*,

sometimes called the *meia-lua* off the southern beach of Caparica, where
they are common. *Meia-lua* means 'half-moon', which aptly describes their
shape. These craft worked off the exposed western beaches all along from
Espinho in the north to Nazare further south, as well as at Caparica. They
were flat-bottomed craft, over 35ft long, canoe-like without a keel that were
launched directly into the surf using huge sweeps, up to 30ft long, each of
which were handled by up to five crew. They had really high prows to enable
them to cope with the large waves of the surf. With four such sweeps being
swung out on the largest craft – some smaller *saveiros* only had two sweeps
– that means there were over twenty crew aboard, and another half-dozen
men helped from the shore by pushing the boat out using another long pole
against the sternpost of the boat, which, incidentally, had no rudder attached.
Often a pair of bullocks was used for this latter task. Once out at sea, the boat
was always rowed, no sails being carried. The boats themselves were used to
set nets a mile offshore, the bridle-ropes of which were then brought back to
the beach, and which were then hauled in onto the beach, again using either
manpower or bullock-muscle. Up to twelve animals were used, taking turns,
to haul in the huge net. Traditionally, the fishermen's wives, the *varinas*, sold
the catch ashore. Indeed, this practise still exists, as I saw myself on several
occasions, both on the markets and from improvised stalls set up around
villages. On one occasion I came across a cart drawn by a tired-looking
horse hawking the day's catch inland of the Ria de Aveiro. Today this means
of fishing has largely disappeared, although I did come across a couple of
saveiros lying idle on the beach at Praia de Mira.

FASSONE REED BOAT FROM SARDINIA

On the West Coast of Sardinia, the fishermen of the Oristano marsh use a one-man raft of two reed-bundles, cut square at the after end, and with the forward end sheering up, the use of which is said to stem from Phoenician influence. The hull thus formed tapers at the forward end and on some rafts a short reed-bundle is fixed on vertically which curves slightly back. This is an advance in construction – a 'beak-head' – and is a separate piece added to the body and is not shown in the example here. The fisherman poles the raft from the aft end and his basket is carried amidships. Reeds are found locally and bundled together in a sufficient density so that they will float for some time before becoming waterlogged. In a warm climate the raft can be used for several hours before being hauled ashore to dry out prior to being used again. They are primarily used to fish for sardines in the shallow water. Similar rafts are used on the Santa Giusta lake, one of the best fishing areas in Sardinia, and in May a feast day is still held there at which time the local gastronomic speciality of *bottarga*, or salted mullet roe, is served.

SWEDISH *EKA*

The *eka* shown here is typical of the type of vessel used on the coast of Hallands and Bohusland in the south-west of Sweden. Sometimes called a *laxeka*, 'lax' meaning salmon, this betrays its normal mode of working the *bottengar* nets – a system of fixed nets set on poles in 10-15ft of water – for salmon. They were worked direct off the beaches and were flat-bottomed like most of the craft here. However, they had vertical sides to work over when at the nets. The uplifted bow, called the *uppnosig*, allowed them to be easily worked off the exposed beaches of Hallands although those worked amongst the islands further north in Bohusland had no need to lift up the bow. Other *eka* are clinker built in a more traditional boat shape, have a flat bottom, centreboard and spritsail and are not unlike the river Parrett flatties. Similarly shaped craft were to be found fishing off the beaches on the eastern side of the country and as far away as the Polish, Estonian, Latvian and Lithuanian beaches.

POLISH CANOES

I've never been to the Polish coast so had to cheat here, lifting the sketch from a book I was once sent. However, over the years I have learned one or two things about the Polish fisheries. It is said that the larger traditional wooden boat types were repressed during the Communist era, the only ones surviving being the small canoes that were incapable of being rowed into deep water and therefore as a means of escape. But that isn't wholly true. Although examples of the older wooden craft are

scarce, there are several museums housing craft. The canoes depicted here are from the river Vistula, the country's major river that flows from the mountains in the south of the country northwards through the capital Warsaw and eventually flowing out into the Gulf of Gdansk and are very different to those of other parts of the country. I simply chose these as a representation of the country's wooden boatbuilding tradition, these belonging to what Jerzy Litwin calls the folk boatbuilding tradition. Similar canoes can be seen on display at the Vistula River Museum at Tczew. On the Vistula Lagoon other sprit-sailed canoes once worked, as did the *zakowka* and *barkas*, examples of which can be seen in the Vistula Lagoon Museum at the town of Katy Rybackie on the western side of the lagoon. Furthermore, at the National Fisheries Museum at Hel, a village at the end of the peninsular of the same name that was noted as being the centre of the herring trade in 1198 and didn't have a harbour built for another 700 years, some eleven traditional vessels can be seen including a *pomeranka*, an offshore sea boat and what appears to be the only remaining example of a drift-net boat. Most of these craft are double-ended, another example being the *heuger* from the mouth of the river Oder.

GREEK *MESOLONGI* CANOES

On the north side of the Gulf of Patra the Mesolongi lagoon is a shallow area where numerous fish weirs are set into the seabed and these canoes were used to service these fish weirs. The small craft are flat-bottomed with simply-shaped sides and many are still in use, although some now are fitted with outboard motors and one or two with inboards. Similar craft –

although seemingly named *pryari* – were used in the Ambracian Gulf further to the north to fish similar weirs. Although dissimilar in design to the typical Greek fishing boats, it is said that they have evolved from influences abounding in the Adriatic so that similar features can be seen today in the Italian *sanaro* and the Croatian *trupa*. I've an idea that the boats in the northern Greek lakes will display similar characteristics but that discovery will have to wait until another time.

BARBATE (SOUTHERN SPAIN) TUNA BOATS

During a tour of the Iberian peninsula in 1999 I came across these double-ended tuna boats situated across the river from the small village of Barbate on the Atlantic side of the South Coast of Spain, some thirty miles from the most southerly point at Tarifa. These long shallow boats, all painted a greyish blue, were similar to the seine-boats I'd seen in the north of the country, and were rowed out in the summer to catch the tuna close inshore. There were several of the boats, and at first I assumed they were leftovers from an ancient age, until one local informed me that they were still used for the tuna fishery, although I'm not sure whether they still are ten years on. I hope so. They seem to have evolved from half-decked boats that operated beach-seines right along into the Algarve region of Portugal. They reminded me of the six traditional tuna boats of the small village of Sidi Daoud, close to Cap Bon in northern Tunisia. Here they still practice the *mattanza*, a method of tuna fishing that dates back to

Roman times, and consists of a series of nets forming separate chambers. Practised only in May and June when the tuna are spawning, the nets, weighing many tons, are laid some two miles offshore from 35ft oared craft so that the fish swim from chamber to chamber until they reach the small chambers from where they are unable to escape. In Tunisia, it is only in Sidi Daoud that this is exercised whilst across the short bit of water they use a similar boat called a *barche di tonnara* at the Sicilian town of Trapani. Once the fish are in the chambers, the dramatic moment of the kill arrives when the fishermen set about the fish with harpoons, clubs and knives to kill them. It is indeed a bloody scene and not for the faint-hearted. Although the Tunisian boats were transom-sterned, the thing that likened one to the other was the way the boats had been taken away from the village to be kept during the off-season. In some strange way it was as if the locals were ashamed of the boats.

LLAGOT FROM SOUTHERN SPAIN

Several miles south of the orange-exporting city of Valencia, on Spain's Mediterranean coast, is the freshwater lake L'Albufera which is renowned for its terrific sunset views and bird life. It was also once home to the *llagot*, a double-ended, flat-bottomed canoe that is now worked under oar. A century ago, though, the lake was much larger but has shrunk due to land reclamation, thus reducing the fisheries, although it is also said that pollution over the last fifty years has also contributed to the loss of fish. Eels were once extremely rich in supply and larger *llagots* worked under a lateen rig but the sailing craft are no longer considered necessary. Today there are said to still be some 400 fishermen catching eels which are cooked locally as *all i pebre de anguilas* – a spicy eel dish. The tradition of having their fishing grounds (*calaes*) assigned on the second Sunday in July by drawing lots still survives as does the *Festa del Cristo de la Salud* on 4 August when a procession of boats carries the crucifix from the church of El Palmar across the lake and back, the boats being covered in flowers. Today many of these boats are motorised and partially decked and used for taking visitors around the lake to see the birds or the sunset. However, whilst passing through a few years ago, I did find several examples of the rowed version of the *llagots*.

GREEK *GAITA*

In parts of Greece, a *gaita* is simply a small double-ended local boat with a flat bottom, usually with a small lateen rig. On the other hand, the island of Hydra, in the Aegean Sea, has its own *gaita*, a small open boat used for fishing. These are unusual in that they have a plumb upright stem and a transom stern, and are about 4–5m long. Other than that, the *gaita* is not particularly of note and is included for that reason – it is simply a regional workhorse boat with nondescript features. For that reason I like them!

DANISH *HAVBAD*

Translating literally to 'sea boat', this boat is amongst the oldest of Danish types. At between 25 and 50ft in length, they had heavily raking stems and sternposts and a small keel and were clinker-built as all the Scandinavian boats of the era were. Normally they were rowed by four, six or sometimes eight oarsmen, depending on their size. In the mid-nineteenth century a small spritsail and jib was added, the craft increasing in size at the same time. They generally worked off the exposed North Sea coast of Denmark, a coast of sandy beaches, sand dunes and a hinterland which was largely barren at that time. The fishermen were part-timers, agricultural labourers and smallholders coming in the spring to camp in huts and staying until the season finished in the autumn. Each camp of fishers had three huts, housing six or eight fishermen, six bait girls who prepared the lines, two baitfishers and one runner who sold the catch which consisted mostly of whitefish. Once the railways arrived in the second part of the nineteenth century the fishing altered drastically, as elsewhere, with much of the catch going direct to Germany.

TUNISIAN CANOE

A couple of years ago whilst travelling along the coast of Tunisia I watched several of these canoe-types return from their morning fishing. Although not in Europe, I include them here because of the proximity to the Sicilian coast, from which influences have been drawn over the centuries, and because I was impressed by their manual dexterity in the way they worked the coast from such an extraordinarily shaped vessel. Built on a flat bottom with the massive amount of rocker, this vessel was unlike anything I'd previously seen. Presumably not working too far out to sea, although that's purely an assumption, the canoe had one central open portion with one thwart for the oarsman and closed compartments at either end. It also had a bracket for an outboard which was left on the beach whilst the boat was carried away from the surf by the two fishermen who came ashore in the boat. Similar, but less extremely shaped, canoe-types were to be seen in many other parts of the Tunisian coast, primarily at Ghar-el-Melh which lies upon a lake of the same name, these canoes being used to fish the lake in contrast to the larger boats there that fished offshore.

WEXFORD COT

The herring cots – from the old Irish *coite* meaning dugout – of today differ considerably from the nineteenth century cots which fished in the limited herring fishery in the shallows off Wexford. Early vessels were about 30ft in length and up to 8ft in beam, old Scandinavian in appearance and yet flat-bottomed except for a small skeg, twin bilge keels and, unusually, a centreboard. They had three spritsails with the mizzen being sheeted to a bumpkin and a small foresail set on a short bowsprit. Today the fishermen of Wexford still use cots although they are smaller than the older craft at around 23ft. These have only one mast and are used for fishing for shellfish in the river or just offshore. They keenly compete in annual regattas with some two dozen boats taking part, although only a few set a sprit whilst the others favour Bermudan or mermaid rigs. However time cannot hide the fact that there is a distinct similarity between these boats and the three-masted craft found only sixty miles across the waters in West Wales. Until very recently 17ft cots, rarely sailed, were used to draft for salmon in the upper reaches of the river Slaney but recent restrictions have prevented any salmon fishing. The same boat is sometimes used for eel fishing although they, like the salmon fishing, are not fished very much at present. The vessel shown is of the latter type, moored in the river and used for pleasure and wildfowling.

ITALIAN *SANARO*

The vessel shown here – called a sanaro or sandolo – was seen at the small harbour of Rodi Garganico on the Promontorio del Gargano in southern Italy in 2002, although many other similar canoes were erratically lying about the beach, some appearing redundant whilst others showed signs of

recent use. These canoe-type vessels were introduced into the local fishery from the nearby lakes of Varano and Lesina. They are flat-bottomed on a slight rocker, light to use and simple and cheap to build. Originally rigged with a small spritsail, those in use today either use oars or an outboard motor. I measured one example and gained some very funny looks from the local fishermen as I cast my tape-measure about the canoe. Whilst doing so at a fairly early hour on the morning after arrival, half a dozen of the craft returned from fishing and landed a box or two of fish direct onto the beach. What is interesting, and visible in the sketch, is the means of construction where the bottom of the boat consists of transverse planking inside, longitudinal planking on the outer skin, and 3in-square frames off the floors supporting double-skinned sides.

FLATNER

Flatners in general come in two types, with the one shown here, sometimes known as the river Parrett flatner, being perhaps the most interesting of the two. The other, often called the Weston-super-Mare flatner, is a typical clinker open boat, probably used as much as a tripping boat off the beach as a fishing boat, and isn't particularly special in any way. Mind you, although I write 'is', the only example I know of lies in the museum at Weston so it's a mute point whether to use the past or present tense! The only characteristic they shared was that both set a spritsail when under sail. The Parrett flatner, though, has enjoyed a renaissance in recent years, thanks largely to *Yankee Jack*, a new flatner built and subsequently launched in 1997 and which has since been sailed right along the Somerset, North Devon and Cornish coasts under the skippership of owner Tony James (see his book *Yankee Jack Sails Again*, published by Seafarer Books, 2006). These boats are simply built on a flat bottom with no keel and are said to have evolved from the dories of the Newfoundland cod fisheries, for some of the large ships working that fishery sailed from these parts. They are general workboats in that small versions – up to 16ft in length – were used on the Somerset levels to carry turf and withies, larger river boats – again of about 16ft – were launched off the steep muddy banks of the river and subsequently fished and the big sea boats – up to 20ft – were sailed around Bridgwater Bay. Some are said to have carried sheep and coal across from South Wales although the majority seem to have fished for mackerel, sprats, salmon and shrimps. At Watchet they were known as 'flatties' where several can be seen in the Watchet Boat Museum including new boats which today are invariably built from plywood instead of elm.

CROMER CRAB BOAT

Cromer has had a fishing fleet since the Middle Ages when 'Clement, Fysheman of Crowmer' left his six-oared boat to his wife Alys and another to his son John. Lobsters and crabs have been the mainstay of this bustling industry although other fish such as herrings and whitefish were obviously landed. In the early part of the nineteenth century the boats these fishermen used were typically Scandinavian in design – double-ended, some 12ft in keel length and rigged with a crude squaresail. During that century they developed, increasing in overall size and adopting a dipping lugsail tacked directly onto the stemhead. Shingle ballast was carried in bags that could be shifted to suit the wind conditions and emptied when coming ashore for, as in many other exposed and harbourless places, they launched and beached directly onto the beach. Thus, like their counterparts the Yorkshire cobles, this dictated their shape of flat in the floors and pointy ends. However, unlike the cobles, they are built on a full keel, initially in clench construction. For ease of carrying them out of the surf, each boat had 'orrucks' or oar ports in the top strake through which the oars could be passed for four fishermen to carry one end of each. Numbers at the end of the nineteenth century were some fifty such boats at Cromer, another 100 at nearby Sheringham – where indeed the vast majority of the pretty little vessels were built – and fifty working from other North Norfolk beaches and inlets. Motorisation impacted upon their shape with an increase in beam but the boats continued in use into the twenty-first century although tractors were the means of pulling them about the beach. On a recent visit to Cromer, though, I found only one traditional crab boat alongside several fibreglass copies, and this one looked pretty redundant!

STOP-NET BOAT

On the lower reaches of the rivers Severn and Wye a particular method of fishing for salmon needed a small boat that could be easily landed yet was strong enough to withstand the strong tide, remembering that this water has the second highest tidal range in the world. The stop-net is a net spread out from two stout wooden poles – or *rames* – that are 'V' shaped so that the net opens up to 30ft in width. When set in the fast current the net and poles were held in place with a prop until a fish was felt to hit the net, at which time the prop was kicked out and the fish hopefully caught. It is believed that the method predates the Civil War in the 1600s. The stop-net boat therefore had to be strongly built and most were built from oak and larch, with ash gunwales, timber coming from the nearby Forest of Dean, once renowned for the quality of its oak. The boats of the river Severn were up to some 26ft in length whilst those of the Wye were a bit smaller. They fished by being moored to wire warps set across the stream or, as on the Wye, by being fixed to poles in the riverbed. In the nineteenth century there were twenty-four boats licenced on the Severn and a further thirty-seven on the Wye. By the 1960s numbers had decreased to three boats on the Severn and

twenty years later all fishing ceased. Luckily several examples of the stop-net boat have survived, a couple in good condition, whilst others have been left to rot by the riverbank. It's worth noting that a similar mode of fishing, albeit with a smaller boat and net, is still practised occasionally on the river Cleddau in Pembrokeshire, where it is known as 'compass-netting'.

SALMON COBLE

Whereas the stop-net boat worked in the relative shelter of a river, on the east coast of Scotland (and other parts for that matter) where the salmon swim parallel to the shoreline on their way back to the river from where they originated, the fishermen lay stake-nets at right-angles to the shore with a bag-net at its outer end. Thus they needed a small open capable of working off the beach, probably in coastal surf conditions and thus the Scottish coble with its defining high prow and transom stern developed. Like the Yorkshire and Northumberland cobles – from which it is likely they developed – they are built on a central ramplank with the flat-bottom planking affixed to this, an apron taking the place of a stem post and a strong transom latterly to support heavy outboard motors. However, in the nineteenth century the cobles were lug-rigged with a drop keel for getting to the stake-nets, although then, as in recent times, they were rowed by the four crew whilst amongst the bag-nets emptying them. Boats, as the fishing stations, were owned by fishing companies with each coble being painted in the chosen colours of that company. Nowadays, with the buy-out of many of the salmon licences to protect the dwindling stocks, rarely are cobles seen at work with modern vessels servicing what nets remain. Those cobles that can be seen are, often as not, relics from a decade or two left to eventually rot.

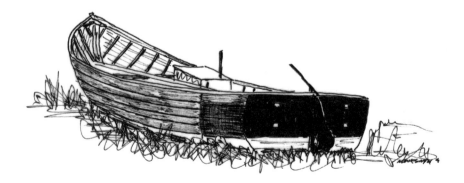

GRIMSAY LOBSTER BOAT

In 2001, two friends and I travelled out to the small island of Grimsay, sandwiched between North Uist and Benbecula in Scotland's Outer Hebrides, at the invitation of Mary Norton to measure up a variety of local fishing boats that had not, hitherto, received much attention from those cataloguing Britain's traditional coastal craft. What I found was a whole world of this particular type of lobster fishing boat that seemed to encapsulate the whole history of the island over the last couple of centuries or so. Although that might sound somewhat pretentious, on a small island such as Grimsay, it cannot be surprising that a home-grown boat for a very local fishery had a major impact upon the lives of the inhabitants. Today, all over the island, and much further afield amongst the Uists and Benbecula, these boats are to be found in hidden corners everywhere, both as rotting shells and happily afloat. Stemming from the need to fish the offshore Monach Islands which are rich in lobster, the double-ended boats were built largely by the Stewart family who originally came to the island in the 1840s from Argyllshire, bringing their design of boat with them. Their design incorporated the need to ride out over surf into deeper water, sail over to the Monachs with enough gear for a week's fishing, haul creels whilst there and return with fishermen and the catch. Rigged with two gaff sails, the fishermen sometimes raced each other home on the Saturday, but while working they left the mizzen mast ashore. As usual, motorisation had its impact upon the type, bringing about a fuller hull shape and a transom, although some boats retained the double-ended influence that is longstanding hereabout. Five generations of the Stewart family worked until recently building boats, and it has been suggested that they built in excess of a thousand. The craft were renowned for their seaworthiness, their lightness and their fineness, especially at their entry, and they were double-enders (*eathar*) until the transom-sterned boats (*geola*) were built. Some of the Stewart boats still survive. The last surviving member, Charles, showed me a boat he was restoring in the old schoolhouse, now owned by Mary Norton who had had him build her her own small version a few years earlier. Largely due to her influence, the inhabitants had rediscovered their own indigenous type of boat, putting what boats were possible back to sea. The boat shown here, the *Lily*, CY173, was found languishing in a bay on the north side of the island and was not one of the eight we took the lines off.

LOCH TORRIDON SKIFF

In the small hamlet of Alligin, on the north shores of Loch Torridon in north-west Scotland, the herring fishery was once all important to the forty crofters who managed to keep one fish curer busy. Three generations of one family of MacDonalds built boats here up to the mid-twentieth century, the last member, Murdo, moving to Papua New Guinea to teach boatbuilding skills to the natives before returning and retiring. The MacDonalds were renowned for small 15ft slightly-built herring skiffs in the 1930s and several of these clinker-built double-ended craft still can be seen around the coasts. This one, slightly smaller in size, I discovered whilst poking about Alligin, primarily to see if the boatshed was still there. It is, albeit as a sort of shop selling fresh vegetables produced locally as well as eggs from hens cackling around the site. One of their larger boats, built in 1910 at a cost of £62, is the *Queen Mary*, UL138, which can be seen at the nearby Gairloch Heritage Centre, and beside this is another of their small skiffs.

RIVER DYFI SEINE-NET BOAT

On many a journey
I drove between North
and South Wales several years
ago I used to espy this small boat lying
in the river Dyfi (Dovey) below the road
at Glandyfi where it becomes extremely narrow and
without a suitable stopping point. One time, though, I made a point
of parking up several hundred yards away and walking up to view the boat
which, luckily, was still anchored at that instance. As I had already surmised, this
was one of the boats used for setting seine-nets in the river for it was a small
rowing boat, probably some 14ft in length, motor boats being prohibited from
use in the fishery. Generally one boat is used by three netsmen, two on the
boat feeding the net out whilst another remains onshore with an end of the
net. The small rowing boats are not unique in any way, just simply a suitable
boat of shallow draft with a shelf at the after end to hold the net. A couple of
years later I watched fishermen set a seine-net in the harbour of Porthmadog
where a similar boat was used. Indeed, although this type of fishing has various
names, and subtle differences between that operated in the confines of a river
and that worked in open estuary, all the boats are generally the same in shape,
albeit larger in deeper waters Thus the draft-net boats of the river Dee are not
indifferent to the salmon boats of the rivers Torridge and Exe in Devon. In
days gone by each boat of an area would have been built by a local boatbuilder,
thus traditions of generations would have survived, but with greater movement
of populations, boats might be imported from anywhere, solely dependent on
price. Regional variations disappear rapidly at this stage.

ST IVES SEINE-NET BOAT

The seine-net was once considered the only way to catch pilchards by the
army of Cornish fishermen that followed the huge shoals until the drift-
net boats gradually gained precedence in the middle part of the nineteenth
century. The operation was carried out by companies of seiners who were
licenced to work a particular area. A seine consisted of three boats, two nets
and an onshore cellar in which to cure the fish. The main boat, as seen here,

was the stop-seiner, an open, low, carvel-built, double-ended vessel of some 35-40ft in length, capable of being rowed by six oars, with the main pilchard net aboard. The second boat was called the 'flyer' or 'tuck-boat' and was generally slightly smaller and carried the second net. The third boat was the 'lurker', much smaller at 16-18ft, and directed the operation from a distance. Sometimes the job of the lurker was dispensed with and the 'huer', stationed on a nearby cliff to spot the shoals, would act as operations director. Using a system of signals, the huer would direct the two larger boats to the shoal and the stop-seine boat would shoot the net around the shoal. Once the net encircled the shoal and the sole ropes tightened to form a sort of bag, the whole lot would be towed into shallower water before the seine was emptied of fish into the boats to be taken ashore. Huge amounts of fish would sometimes be taken at one go: in the autumn of 1851 one single seine is said to have captured 17,908,800 pilchards that took a week to land and realised a massive £7,500 – the equivalent of about £750,000 in today's figures. Today what pilchards are caught off the south coast of Cornwall are largely taken with a ring-net, a net that can be said to work in somewhat the same way, albeit worked from a single vessel.

RIVER LUNE WHAMMEL-NET BOAT

At Sunderland Point, on the northern shore of the river Lune, the fishermen developed their own way of fishing for salmon. This involved shooting a gill-net that is staked at one end close to the shore, deploying it across the main stream of the river and back to the shore in a wide arc, before hauling it in. For this – called whammel-netting, something similar to draft-netting on the river Dee – a 20ft whammel boat was developed from the Crossfield-built mussels boats used on the river and estuary. These whammel boats had a sloping transom and were rigged with a standing lugsail. A foresail was sometimes set on a very short bowsprit, although most fishermen tended not to bother with this. By the beginning of the twentieth century these whammel boats became more identifiable in their own right, with some sixteen boats working from Sunderland Point and Glasson Dock, where an unofficial co-operative existed enabling both groups of men to co-exist without problems. Most of these boats had been built by Jack Woodhouse at his yard in Overton a couple of miles from Sunderland Point. The 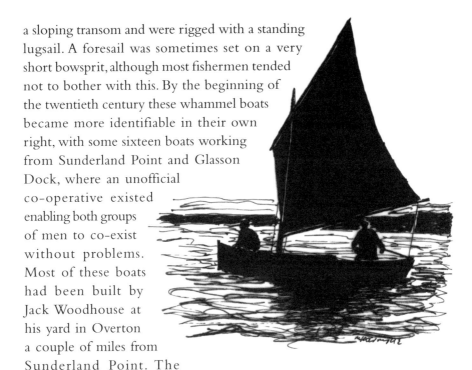 Woodhouse family had been building boats here since 1660, the last one being the *Mary*, LR 53, in 1937. She was built for Tom Smith's father and is named after his mother. Tom is one of the few fishermen still fishing from Sunderland Point and has another Woodhouse boat, the *Sirius*, LR 33, built in 1923 for James 'Shirley' Gardner and Tommy Spencer.

CORACLES

The best description of a coracle is a small keel-less, bowl-shaped, one-man fishing boat made from a timber framework with either hide or canvas stretched tautly over. Although several Roman writers mentioned small skin-covered vessels it is doubtful whether they were referring to coracles as against larger sea-going craft of the Irish currach type. Coracles appear to have developed purely to fish in fast-flowing rivers and mention was made of them in the Dark Ages although it was Giraldus Cambrensis (known as Gerald of Wales) who journeyed through Wales in 1188 and noted boats made out of willow and covered in raw hides 'almost circular or rather in the form of a triangle'. As the drawings here suggest, the Welsh coracles come in a variety of shapes. However, coracles are to be found on some of the Irish and Scottish rivers, and in parts of the river Severn that lie in England. Other well-known users of skin-covered craft are to be found in Iraq, Vietnam and India: some years ago we were ferried across the river at Hampi, southern India in a coracle of about 8ft in diameter with several other passengers. Coracles have over the last two decades been built by numerous folk, mostly using ash and canvas, although a few builders use traditional materials. Peter Faulkner of Leintwardine, Shropshire is perhaps the best known of these, using his own grown hazel and willow and self-cured hides to build his Teme coracles and a larger Boyne model. He has also built several hide-covered currachs which have been sailed in the open sea.

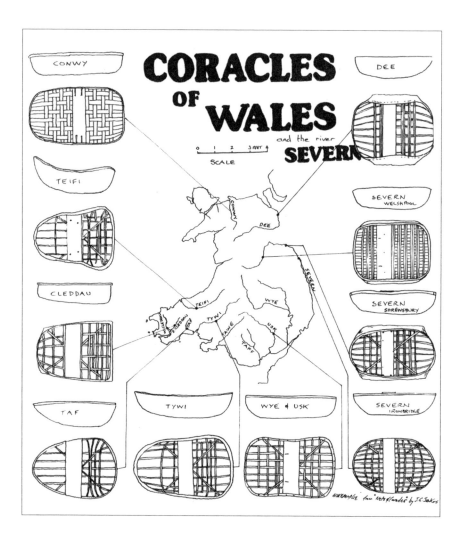

THREE

SAILING CLOSE TO
THE SHORE

INTRODUCTION

Between the sandy shore and the deep blue sea there is a huge zone in the vernacular where the boats out fishing are capable in a limited way of working off the beach yet are also able to sail some distance away from the land. The vast proportion of their working life, though, is spent close to the shore and the vast majority of them do not work directly off beaches. However, as in most cases there are exceptions, as in the Dutch *bomschuit*, a clumsy squat vessel that works off the beaches in proximity to the North Sea coast of Scheveningen and Katwijk, yet often works as far away as the Shetland Isles as several photographs of the time support. However, as it fits into neither the previous chapter, nor the next, it is included in this one.

Some of these sailing boats survived the transition from sail to motor that began, in the case of the fishing fleets, in the first decade of the twentieth century although some European countries were slow to benefit from the change. On the other hand some vessels were not suited to receiving stern tubes through their sternposts. Some, such as the Lochfyne skiffs of the Clyde and surrounding area, found that the early petrol/paraffin engines of low horsepower could be fitted to one side with strengthening blocks placed inside and outside around where the stern tube exited. These early engines were highly unreliable so that the rig was retained, perhaps shortened a bit. However, as engine performance improved over the next two decades, the rig disappeared and the hull shape altered, adapted to carry the increasingly powerful units.

Some of these boats such as the Croatian *gajeta falkusa* all but disappeared from our shores until replica vessels were built. On the other hand others such as the Dutch *hoogaarzen*, have survived in considerable numbers. Several years ago I travelled over to the annual mussel festival in Antwerp, sailing aboard one *hoogaars* as the fleet of these boats and Dutch *botters* sailed up the river into the centre of the city. It was a fine sight, one that is often seen today with the increasing number of restored or replicated vessels at various festivals around the country. I write this having just returned from the biennial 2007 Looe Lugger regatta where some fifty-four luggers assembled, along with a few gaffers, to race around the bay. Again it was a formidable sight. But in Europe the largest assembly of these craft occurs every four years when traditionalists from all over the continent voyage to Brest for a massive sail to Douarnenez. In terms of the sea, the spectacle of over a thousand vessels of all types, with a rainbow of coloured sails, moving slowly and gently across Douarnenez Bay, is unbeatable.

GERMAN *GIEKEWER*

Ewer translates to 'boat driven by one man' and relates to a small fishing boat of the lower river Elbe. These adopted a square sail and became known as *pfahlewer* or 'pole-mast ewers'. Flat-bottomed double-enders with a hard chine, these boats developed from the basic three-plank boat with the hull being raised up in carvel build, the original bottom part becoming the wet-well. These fished in the river and later worked as pilot boats from the growing ports of Cuxhaven and Hamburg. But by 1860 Finkenwerder, close to Hamburg, had become the chief fishing port on the river to feed the increasing population of that city and these fishermen were amongst the first to use the new trawl. For this they adopted the gaff rig, and the boats themselves subtlety changed and became known as *giekewers* – *gieg* being the main boom – adding a topsail and jib. The *giekewer* shown here has the typical rounded stem and heavily sloping sternpost with large rudder, so typical of the boats of the Low Countries and Friesland. By 1870 the fishermen had added a second mast, enabling them to sail further afield and to tow a larger trawl. Other ewers were used for carrying fruit (*fruitewers*), bricks (*stonewers*) and larger cargoes (*galeasewers*). As far as I know the only surviving fishing ewer is the *Maria*, HF31, built in 1869 and now in the Deutsche Museum in Munich, although a couple of replicas have been built.

DUTCH *BOMSCHUIT*

This I think is probably one of the more extraordinary boats of Europe. The outstanding feature of this beach-based craft was the 2:1 length to breadth ratio, making it look dumpy and squarish in appearance, and on deck it was literally a rectangle with the corners rounded off. Based on the sandy beaches of Scheveningen and Katwijk, they were built locally. Fishing hereabouts dates back at least to the fourteenth century when the fish market at Katwijk, according to records, was moved to the sea village. Fishing, though, was the domain for the poor until a thriving smuggling trade developed in the seventeenth century. The Monopoly Act was introduced to counter this, by which only square-rigged keeled boats were allowed to fish the North Sea herring which the Dutch commanded at the time. Thus the *bomschuiten* and foreign boats were unable to fish. The villagers continued illegally, selling their fish outside the village and, when the

Act was repealed in 1857, fishing became profitable. Although they appeared pretty clumsy, these boats were seaworthy and often sailed as far as northern Scotland and the Shetland Islands. They were mostly built at four yards in Katwijk, the best known being W. Taat's two covered yards. However, being beach-based, they had to be turned around for launching, and a large corkscrew apparatus was attached to one end to lift it in the air whilst horses and manpower were used to pull the vessel around 180 degrees. Being beach-based also was often the cause of their demise through both hard wear and North Sea storms. In 1894 a storm destroyed twenty-five vessels from the Scheveningen fleet and damaged another 150, leading to the building of the harbour there. Katwijk had no harbour and accordingly lost its fleet to Scheveningen. However, after some arguments, the 1911-built *bomschuit* KW88 was returned to Katwijk and now sits outside the lighthouse there as a reminder of the hundreds of these vessels that once worked these coasts.

CROATIAN *GAJETA FALKUSA*

This vessel is said to have originated from the island of Vis, one of the nearest islands to Palagruza, a small island with a lighthouse situated out in the middle of the Adriatic and in the richest fishing area in the whole Adriatic, although the fishermen also fished the nearer islands of Svetac and Jabuka. It is a forty-two-mile journey from Vis to Palagruza so the fishermen, in venturing out when the north-west *maestral* wind was blowing, had to take with them a full load of salt to cure their sardines once they were caught. Thus their boats had to be capable of carrying a heavy cargo of fishing gear, salt and men. Once at the island, if the moon was new, fishing could begin. Here they needed a light boat, easily manoeuvred with five oars, with low freeboard to set and haul their gill-nets. Once the fish was landed, and salted ashore, they had to wait for the *jugo* wind from the south to sail home fully laden. Thus the *gajeta falkusa* evolved over time to suit their purposes. To the normal light vessel are added the *folke* or *falke*, detachable washboards that increase the freeboard. These and the mast and bowsprit are fixed using rope and dowels, and the cross-beams temporarily removed to allow salt to be packed beneath. Once they have arrived at Palagruza, the *folke*, rig, rudder, barrels of salt, wine and water – everything that gets in the way of net handling – gets left ashore until the return journey and they solely use the oars whilst fishing. There's a tradition that the fishermen, during their long expeditions to the islands, used to climb the steep rocks to collect firewood for cooking their sardines, whilst at the same time collecting wild carnations for their sweethearts back home. This they had to keep secret as the older men forbade it, believing the ancient prophecy that the fishing

would perish if the carnation disappeared from the rock of Jabuka. They did, eventually, and the fishing, which finished in 1936, was said to have lasted a thousand years. Most of the ancient *gajetas* were burnt during the festival of St Nicholas on 6 December each year as a tribute to the bounty from the sea. Fortunately one *gajeta* had survived after being damaged in a storm in 1988 and beached. This, the *Cicibela*, was surveyed and the lines lifted to enable the replica to be built in the shipyard at Trogir, on the mainland west of Split. At 9m in length, 2.9m in breadth and with a 9m-high mast, the vessel was built using pine from the island of Svetac although the keel is oak. Authenticity was insisted upon at every stage so that distilled pine resin (*katram*) was applied to protect the hull and spars from decay. The replica vessel was launched in 1997 and named *Comeza-Lisboa* for she was built in time to appear at the EXPO 98 in Lisbon. Two years later she appeared at the Brest maritime festival where I was lucky enough to have seen her. In 1999 she returned to Palagruza and fished in the age old way, under oars, as a one-off.

DUTCH *HOOGAARS*

Around the estuaries of Zeeland, in the south of Holland, and around the waters of Antwerp in Belgium, the *hoogaars*, a flat-bottomed vessel rigged with one boomless spritsail, was developed. Sometimes called a Flushing mussel boat, this describes part of their work in latter years, although initially they were used for all manner of work – freight, ferrying and fishing. Apart from mussel dredging, they also fished for shrimps. Being flat, they were easy to beach in the mud, but there were degrees of flatness which characterises *hoogaarzen* from different areas. Thus those from Duiveland in the north had completely flat bottoms whilst those from Arnemuiden on Zeeland itself were deeper draughted, being deepest at a point below the mast and curving up to only a few inches at the waterline fore and aft. Some had a wet-well whilst most had a shrimp boiler. All had leeboards, were built of oak on oak and consequently had a long working life even if they did constantly scrape along the rough seabed in the harsh conditions of their working life. At the end of the nineteenth century it is said that the waters around Zeeland were simply teeming with these vessels. In recent years, in common with many other Dutch working vessels, many have been adapted as pleasure boats which, in turn, has led to some traditional types now being built in modern materials.

GERMAN *BUTTEJOL*

This is another fishing boat from the river Elbe – literally a 'sole yawl'. These double-enders had a large, flat sternpost with a big out-hung rudder, a high, round stem and wide planking. At about 16ft in length until the mid-nineteenth century, the largest from the lower river set a squaresail with, unusually, two reef points at the top, on a single pole mast. A storm mast was carried in case of adverse weather when working in the estuary or open sea. In the second half of the century, though, some of the *buttejols* were built half-decked with a cuddy and a wet-well amidships, increasing in size at the same time. At some time in the 1880s the lug rig was introduced as is shown on the vessel here. The boats were fished by one man and a boy using tangle nets and a small punt was kept close so that the nets could be emptied on the mud banks. As far as I know, only one original *buttejol* has survived, this having been converted into a motorboat.

MALTESE *FERILLA* AND *SPERONARA*

The *ferilla* is said to have been the first Maltese fishing boat, originating from small rowing boats used in Grand Harbour. The first fishermen of the fifteenth century were regarded as being shopkeepers who went fishing, only to return with more than their families could eat, so the surplus was sold off in their shops. Thus, as they needed to sail further offshore, their boats became bigger in the eighteenth century, rigged with a spritsail. These were double-ended and were somewhat similar to the *speronara*, the first trading boats that worked between North Africa, Malta and Italy but that originated from Gozo, although there are distinct similarities to the Sicilian craft. Malta was first settled by Sicilian hunter gatherers in about 5000BC and later both islands were under the same Arab rule, so comparisons between their native vessels is not unreasonable. During the nineteenth century the *ferilla* developed into a popular fishing vessel which appeared all over the island built by a multitude of builders all of whom had been trained in the naval shipyards of Grand Harbour, where the highest concentration of builders sprung up for obvious reasons – acquiring timber from the yards, preferably free! All the boats, renowned for their speed, were brightly painted, and all had removable washboards – *falki* – which were removed when setting the nets yet slid back into place when sailing. The boats also had a *sperone*, a protrusion fixed onto the cutwater at the bow as a form of decoration, as well as the Eye of Osiris to ward off evil spirits. This in fact is what gave the *speronara* their name, and is said to have come from Arabic influence. At the beginning of the twentieth century the small port of Marsaxlokk became the main fishing harbour of the islands and consequently was full of the *ferilli*. However, when motors were introduced to the Maltese fleets in the 1920s, the *ferrilla* was found unsuitable to receive them and a new breed of motor fishing boat, the *luzzu*, appeared. More of these later.

GOZO BOAT

The Gozo boat appeared about 1880, superseding the *speronara* almost immediately. These boats were much deeper than the shallow, flat-bottomed earlier craft, and were up to 40 tons, built by the same boatbuilders who were building the *ferilli*. Again they had bright paintwork and detachable washboards and rigged with two lateen sails and jib. Although built primarily to transport goods from Grand Harbour over to Mjarr, Gozo's main harbour, some did fish. They worked well with motors and survived long after the Second World War, although only a few examples still existed when I visited Gozo several years ago.

WARNEMUNDE *JOLLE*

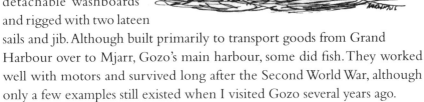

The sprit-rigged *jolles* from Warnemunde on the eastern side of the Mecklenburger Bucht, near Rostok on the Baltic Sea, come in three different sizes – the *Volljolle* (22-24ft), the *Dreivierel jolle* (20ft) and the single-masted *Halbjolle* (16-18ft). Except for their size, these open keeled boats are very similar to the *smakkejolles* of southern Denmark and *jolles* of the Eckernfjord to the west. Some of these boats carried three masts although generally the Warnemunde boats had two. They were used for all manner of fishing, and even pilotage and ferrying work. The main fishing they attended was the annual mackerel and herring.

GOZZO OF SORRENTO

The *gozzo* was a type of boat to be found almost all over the West Coast of Italy, from the Ligurian Riviera in the north to Sicily in the south. They were also to be found around the Gulf of Naples, where they were known as *gozzi di Sorrento*. This was a much sharper and narrower boat than its counterpart to the north, very flat and without sheer, although the body section was full and almost flat-bottomed. They were sprit-rigged with a jib on a long bowsprit. They were seldom longer than 25ft. One example discovered recently on the beach at Cetera, on the Amalfi coast, which was not rigged like these two shown, but was just as distinctive. However, *gozzi* were also prevalent amongst the islands of Capri and Ischia, and the other villages of the picturesque Amalfi coast. One interesting development of the *gozzo* was the *barca di Ponza*, from the island of that name in the Tyrrehian Sea, where the inhabitants were of those fishing off Sardinia. This boat, about 33ft in length, had an upright stem with the stern being an almost cleverly-designed cross between a cruiser stern and the straight sternpost, the space in between being filled with a large propeller aperture. In profile the vessel reminded me of the Scottish motor *fife*. However, the similarity ends there, for the floors are deeper and the boat less beamy

ITALIAN *LANCIA*

The *lancia Romagnola* has been in the past referred to as the Ancona fishing boat for its true origins come from around that region and its usage never penetrated further north than Romagna. It is said that it represents one of the most recent types of traditional Italian fishing craft yet, in terms of hull decoration when compared with craft from Venice, it was one of the most restrained. The typical *lancia* is about 30ft long, 7ft in the beam, flat-bottomed for easy beaching with some 2ft of draft, and has a single lugsail and two foresails set on a bowsprit. Whilst visiting the region, I found two prime examples at Cervia. The *Assunta* was built in 1925 at Patrignani di Cattolica and has been fitted with a Farriman Diesel 18hp motor. The other, the *Maria*, was also built at Cattolica, which is between Rimini and Pesaro, in 1949. Both have brightly coloured sails with individual patterns upon that are unique to each fisherman. Usually they represent holy scenes and are to enable those on shore to identify the returning boats. Another, the *Saviolina*, was also built in Cattolica and is today sailed from Riccione. Cesanatico lies a bit south of Cervia and is also home to a fleet of these craft. Thus the summer races are keenly competed, with each saying their craft are the finest. Each year they join in with the 'manifestation of the fishery' at which time the boats sail from Cervia with a local priest or bishop aboard who, once the company is assembled, throws a ring into a group of swimming youngsters. If the ring is caught, the fishery will be bountiful and, if not, some don't even bother. In 1986 the Pope came to officiate with the ring and the ring was caught. At his visit he sailed out upon a *bragozzo*. This tradition reaches back to 1545 and continues today on the first Sunday in June.

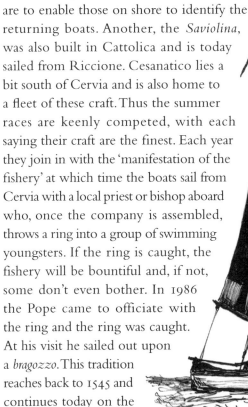

NORWEGIAN LISTA BOAT

Norwegian destiny has always been to the sea for some two-thirds of its population live almost upon it. The Lista boat was the archetypical boat of the southern part of the country in the days of sail and oar, Lista itself being a small town close to the southern point of the country. I've seen the same boat referred to as a *snaekke* or skiff, but they are all the same open boats, built in the true Norwegian style with rounded stems and sternposts. Originally square-sailed, they adopted the sprit-rig and were used for all manner of work around the southern fjords, fishing, piloting and transporting. Although the one shown is open, they were decked over in the late nineteenth century and the most characteristic type has been said to be the Hvalor-boat which is closely related to the Swedish and Danish Baltic craft that so influenced Colin Archer is his design work and for which the shape of these boats he made famous.

NORWEGIAN NORDFJORD BOAT

The fishing boats of the north of Norway are very different and display similar characteristics of the Viking longships so talked about in history. They are clinker-built, double-ended open craft with a low freeboard amidships and high ends, and continued with the square rig much longer than elsewhere, adding a square topsail. They supposedly had fantastic sea-keeping qualities which they must have inherited from the longships if they sailed so far on their travels, even reaching North America if the Sagas are to be believed and which seems quite plausible. It has been suggested that the secret of these Nordlands boats lies in the lightness of the ends so that, although they are lively in any

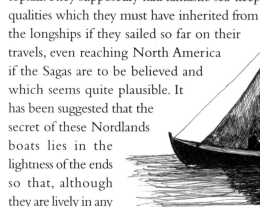

sea, are extremely handy to manoeuvre. The seamen must have been extremely experienced to make them seaworthy because of their narrowness and the squareness of their rig although they were as often as not rowed by up to eleven oarsmen. They were generally used for herring and cod fishing, the latter being centred around the Lofoten Islands where a rich cod fishery still exists.

N. DENMARK *JOLLE*

I suppose it is fair to say that the *jolle*, typical of northern Denmark, is an improvement upon the earlier beach-based *havbad*, still double-ended but rigged with two sprits and topsails. They were a common boat working close inshore in both the Skagerrak and Kattegat, and were similar to many of the craft found on the West Coast of Sweden. I include them here as a representation of the many different subtleties amongst the Danish boats fishing these waters, including the herring boats from the north of Zeeland, the Oresund boats, the Klitmoller *jolles* with their transom sterns and the *belt-jolles*, some of which became gaff rigged.

SWEDISH *VASSING*

Here we see the basic Swedish version of a *jolle*, and it is obviously comparable to the previous boat. The one shown here was from Varberg on the eastern side of the Kattegat and is slightly larger than the typical Swedish *snipa* that was used for all manner of fishing – small net fishing, lobstering and using a *ryssja* net for catching eels. Unlike the sprit-rigged *snipa*, the *vassing* set a high-peaked gaff, topsail and two foresails. Generally, in fine Scandinavian tradition, all these vessels were clinker constructed.

SPANISH *LANCHA*

A couple of years ago I came across a book by Staffan Morling entitled *Lanchas and Dornas* (published by Batdokgruppen, 2003) which subtitled itself as 'cultural stability and boat shape on the west coast of Galicia'. As a study of regional boat types it must stand out as one of the best works in the field. I'd seen some *dornas* during my circumnavigation of the Iberian peninsular in 1999 without coming across any of the *lanchas* but was immediately taken with them on reading the book. They were developed for the sardine fishery, working close to the shore for there never was much need to venture far out to sea, the grounds around the north-west of Spain being among the richest in Europe, until recent times. It's a double-ended boat with a sharp, raked stem and sternpost and the vessel was said to be almost symmetrical. Indeed, according to Morling, when motorisation came many owners converted the stern to the bow and had the original bow altered to receive a stern tube. The average length of a *lancha* was around 25ft, and most had fore and side decks although the area of these was increased after motorisation. They were often called *lanchas de relinga* which referred to the particular sail – *vela de relinga* – a form of the lugsail that is set on a short yard on a mast that has an adjustable raking that lowers the centre of sail area, thus improving performance. Although the *lancha* survived well into the twentieth century as a workboat, it was regarded as a heavy boat and, although smaller and lighter and built in fibreglass, the *buceta* of the Galician coast has similar lines to the older *lancha*.

BELGIUM *SCUTE*

My first glimpse of a *scute* was from the harbour wall, looking down onto this remarkable vessel. Bluff, square and incredibly beamy, this was the ancient fishing vessel of Blankenberge, although the *scute* in question had only recently been built – launched on 12 September 1999 to be exact. The last working boat was built in 1915 and this, along with the other fifty-odd working there up to the First World War, had been destroyed by the Kaiser. Another sixty-odd vessels worked off the beach at Heist, a stone's throw to the east of Zeebrugge. These, too, suffered the same untimely fate.

Named the *St Pieter* after the patron saint of fishermen, she was the brainchild of Daniel Bosser, himself an ex-fish salesman, and the project had taken him and his partners eight years to realise. The lines came off a model that had been commissioned by the Church and still existed in the townhouse, a model stemming from the annual traditional procession, when fishermen carried models of their craft high on their shoulders onto the beach and the priest blessed the sea to ensure a fruitful year's fishing. Seven years hard working followed for Daniel, usually on Sundays and Mondays, battling with huge lumps of oak and elm, of which the boat is built. Although constructional techniques are similar to general practice, there are several differences. The backbone is oak, the keel itself being laid flat, 18in wide and just over 3in deep. The frames are fixed onto this, these being massive for the 40ft vessel – almost 4in x 4in doubled, spaced 8in apart. A keelson, three internal bilge stringers and the beamshelf were then fixed and bolted, the frames being notched for the former. Only then can the laborious job of planking begin. When you see the vessel you see just how much bend the 18in x 1in planks of elm need. Daniel used a fire beside a steel framework to bend them, throwing water on the plank continuously while the plank is forced around metal cross-bars to shape. Each plank took a day to bend and fix. One of the basic differences between the Blankenberge and Heist *scute* is apparent here. The former has four bottom planks laid side by side in carvel fashion, followed by five clinker planks. The Heist craft are all clinker built. Then, once these are in place, the bulwarks can be added onto stanchions bolted through the beamshelf. A cuddy in the bows has four very low bunks that the fishermen would use while whiling away the hours drifting to their nets. Another difference between the boats of the two towns is the rig. The Heist boats have a single gaff sail in Dutch fashion while the Blankenberge craft have two dipping lugs in the French style. And the latter are renowned for the extremely forward-raking foremast in the eyes of the boat, although over the centuries this became more upright. St Pieter's stands as vertical as the larger mainmast that sits against one of the three chunky transverse thwarts that strengthen the whole vessel. What makes these craft so remarkable is the beam and the draft – 16ft and 2ft respectively. Extreme for a 40ft boat in anyone's book. Two stout oak leeboards counteract this. There's a definite feeling of the history of this craft once aboard. The only modern clutter – navigation gear and the such – is hidden away so that even the VHF aerial is brought out and put on the rail only when at sea. The only exception is the sound of the engine!

FRENCH FLOBARD

The flobard of the northern French coast of Picardie – between Cap Gris Nez and Berck-sur-Mer – is a direct result of the Vikings settling the area in the eighth century and are almost identical to the beach boats of Sussex. Similarly flat-bottomed to work off the beaches, the boats as they have been in recent times first appeared in the seventeenth century with the rig being a result of dropping the third mast. They had very upright stems, deep hulls, sloping transoms and a pronounced sheer line. But in about 1850 they were one of the few boats to have a centre-board as previously they had been considered pretty unstable. Most were up to some 20ft in length, with larger boats working out of Berck and Etaples for the herring, the largest of these being 42ft and 30 tons. In Wissant, to the north, they were under 20ft in length. By 1925 motors were being installed in the flobards so that today they can still be found along certain parts of the beach. A similar vessel is the *vaquelotte* of Normandy, the small carvel-built rowing and sailing attending boats.

IRISH TOWELSAIL YAWL

The lobster boats of Roaringwater Bay in County Cork voyaged anywhere between Dursey Head at the end of the Beara peninsular to Ardmore in County Waterford in their search for lobsters and crayfish, staying out usually about a week and sometimes two. Thus the 'towelsail' name comes from their habit of sleeping below a tent erected over the bow of the boat, called a *teabhal* in the local Irish dialect which, for some reason, became confused with the English word 'towel'. Ranging generally between 24 and 28ft in length, there were several builders of these gaff-rigged open boats. I had the pleasure of sailing aboard the only remaining original lobster boat, the *Hanorah*, S463, first built in 1892 by Richard Pyburn of Heir Island and rebuilt in the first years of this century and owned by Nigel Towse of Sherkin Island. Racing in the Baltimore Regatta Week, we beat the other three lobster boats sailing, including Cormac Levis' boat *Saoirse Muireann*. Cormac is the author of the widely acclaimed book *Towelsail Yawls – The Lobsterboats of Heir Island and Roaringwater Bay* and, along with Nigel and Oldcourt boatbuilder Liam Hegarty, was responsible for the resurgence in their popularity and the subsequent building of five replicas.

CLOVELLY HERRING BOAT

A couple of years ago I was lucky enough to meet Stephen Perham from Clovelly whilst recording a programme on herring for BBC Radio 4's *Food Programme*. Although there has been much rubbish written and said about the fishing boats of Clovelly, Stephen, it seemed, was the first person to speak sense. There have been, in general, three types of fishing boat working out of Pool Quay, the small picturesque harbour there – the herring boats, the long-boomers and picarooners. The best known of the long-boomers, stoutly built carvel smacks with characteristic long booms overhanging the sterns, was *Teazer*, 218BD, which was built by R. Blackmore of Appledore in about 1880. However, although she has been described as a typical long-boomer, it appears 'she was meant for a little yacht', according to Jesse Dunn in 1947. He had owned her, and his father before him, and they both beam-trawled with the boat. He further described her as 'a pretty little cutter, with a flat bottom, like a herring boat, body pretty full and a tiny stern. For Clovelly Quay Pool she had bilge-keels, about five inches deep.' That suggests to me that the *Teazer* was not typical and she was eventually ripped up at Barnstaple in 1942. As for the picarooner, she is a small open boat of about 17ft, of which there are several around. The Clovelly herring boat, now, is elusive. One is shown in E. W. White's *British Fishing-Boats and Coastal Craft* from the Science Museum. This is the 19.2ft *Rattling Jack*, built by Captain John Mills of Clovelly in 1886 of oak obtained from the woods above the village. She is shown as being bluff with a near vertical transom and very deep sternpost. She was decked forward, with wide waterways which continued right aft. The rig was a large dipping forelug and standing mizzen lug. However, Stephen gave me a folder with lots of information on the herring boats. The *Pearl* was one of the last built and last to disappear and, at 24ft overall, one of the largest ever built. She was built in 1883 in Bideford at a yard by the bridge (possibly another Blackmore, grandson of the above) and ended her days rotting away in a creek on the river Taw. Although 20ft was the typical length of a Clovelly herring boat, they were renowned as being staunch and beautiful vessels, and very seaworthy. According to James Whitfield who worked upon the building of *Pearl* as an apprentice and was still building in 1935, they were all built of local oak except for the elm keel. They had flat floors to sit in the harbour, sharp ends with a lovely heart-shaped or wine-glass transom. *Pearl* started off life as a lugger but she was subsequently re-rigged as a cutter. Presumably this was because the picaroons had already appeared by the time she had been built so she didn't survive long at the herring. Under cutter-rig she was used for taking trippers out in summer, trawling at Ifracombe and Clovelly and then, in 1926, she spent seven years or so barging gravel in the river Taw before being left in Fremington Pill, where she fell apart.

BEER LUGGER

Down on the stony beach on Beer, along the eastern edge of Devon's south coast, lie some nine lug-rigged open boats, set apart from the modern fishing craft and wooden tripping boats. Although not all the boats are original luggers that worked off the beach, they are rigged as such and enjoy racing around the bay on Monday evenings during the summer. The men of Beer were amongst the first to adopt the trawl-net, although they were working out of Brixham at the time. Is it at their door, then, that we must lay the blame for trawling? At Beer itself, where fishing and smuggling went hand in hand, the men used little three-masted luggers for herring and mackerel drifting, lining for mackerel and potting for crabs and lobsters. The last of these three-masters was the *Beatrice Annie*, E80, which fished until being broken up in 1918. A couple of years earlier the first lugger – the third mast had been generally dropped by then – had been fitted with a Brit engine from nearby Bridport. The luggers were in use all along this coast, from Sidmouth to Westport, and motorisation had the same effect as elsewhere else: the boats became fuller and the rig was eventually dispensed with. In 1985 local fisherman's son (and believed ancestor of local renowned smuggler Jack Rattenbury) Alan Abbot rekindled interest in the luggers by forming, with others, the Beer Luggers Club. At first only a handful of luggers joined in the regatta but as enthusiasm increased, so did the number of boats out racing. I spoke to Alan recently when he showed me the nine boats on the beach including his own *Sea Witch*, and counted another eight that he said either did race or would soon be able to. So, as the saying goes, 'Beer made Brixham, Brixham made the North Sea'. The question is, did the Beer men foresee the damage that their trawling would do to fish stocks generally? If so, maybe they are trying to make amends by reinstating the tradition of racing their boats. I think not!

CORNISH PILCHARD DRIVER

In the last chapter we saw how drifting for pilchards superseded the older seining. Thus evolved the pilchard driver – 'driver' from the act of driving the fish into the net – a half-decked lugger of about 30ft in length. Most were transom sterned in the Cornish fashion although some of the St Ives and Mounts Bay boats were double-ended to fit snugly into drying harbours. Larger drivers were used for the mackerel fishery, bigger because they had to sail into deeper water and often sailed over to the Kinsale mackerel fishery and even to the North Sea herring fishery. The Cornish luggers were principally built in St Ives, Newlyn, Porthleven, Mevagissey, Fowey and Looe although there were other builders. One of the best known was William Paynter of St Ives who not only built craft for Cornwall, but was recognised for his fine craft through the Irish Sea, most notably in south-west Scotland, the Isle of Man and parts of the eastern coast of Ireland. Paynter himself moved his business over to Kilkeel in 1875 after the Manx fishers had adopted his design as their 'nickeys'. Sensing a booming trade, he was disappointed even though he built several luggers as the Manx builders undercut him in price and a disastrous fire gutted his premises within a year of setting up the business. He did recover sufficiently to build a few more luggers but in 1883 gave up and returned to Cornwall leaving his apprentice John MacKintosh behind to carry on. The drivers survived the motorisation

stage for they worked well under power. In Looe a few luggers continued working into the 1970s although their working days were about to finish. However, with many converted to pleasure and, over the years, more and more cropping up, there are today a good number of the boats still afloat, a few even working as charter boats although the vast majority are owned by enthusiasts. As I mentioned earlier, some fifty-four luggers turned up to the 2007 Looe Lugger regatta, most emanating from Cornwall, and that in poor weather when many were put off by the forecast.

HASTINGS LUGGER

Today the dark-coloured tall net houses are amongst the distinctive landmarks of Hastings and the beach below them still has the remnants of a fishing industry working directly off the beach. However, with recent upheavals within the industry, the fleet is severely depleted from even a decade ago. However, of those that do remain, a few betray the shape of the traditional boats that Hastings is well known for. The first documented Hastings luggers were three-masted, many built close to the beach by boatbuilders George

Tot and Robert Kent, the latter beginning building in 1835. Similar luggers worked from beaches all along the Sussex coast, and further afield. By the middle of the century the foremast had been discarded but the fishing went into decline until the railway arrived in the town in 1851. Trawling then began in earnest and a smaller lugger of about 28ft evolved, specifically suited to trawling although they also drifted for the autumn herring. In 1892 the first elliptical-sterned lugger, the *Clupidae*, RX126, arrived, the stern being influenced from successful yachting designs. Previous to that many of the luggers had lute sterns but the elliptical was deemed better for in a following sea as the water tended to flood up around the rudder post. Both sterns had been designed to make running ashore and launching into the surf safer by allowing the oncoming wave to run smoothly over the surface of the boat rather that smashing against a transom. This elliptical stern gained precedence so that, excepting the modern designs now seen on the beach, the motorised 'luggers' (they carry no sail) exhibit the same shape. The last true sailing lugger built was the *Enterprise* in 1912 and those built subsequently were fitted with motors so that they were fuller in shape. Today the *Enterprise* is exhibited in the Hastings Fishermen's Museum while the 1919-built motorised lugger *Edward and Mary* now stands outside the museum. Well, at least the two boats were there the last time I was, but that was a few years ago!

SHETLAND SIXAREEN

Of all British fishing craft, the sixareens are probably the ones nearest to their Viking ancestors, largely due to the Shetlands Isles remaining part of the Norse Kingdom until 1469, at which time they were returned to Scottish rule as part of the dowry of a Danish princess to her betrothed Scotsman. Incredible, isn't it, to think that a group of islands can be treated in such a way. Mind you, that didn't stop exploitation over the next 500 years or so, and the sixareens were part of this abuse in that the landowners forced generations of their tenants to sail out in their sixareens to long-line for whitefish, sometimes thirty or forty miles offshore. In return, they paid them in vouchers only redeemable in their own shops. If they refused, the family were evicted from their family homes. And it wasn't until the

1872 Truck Report that things began to change. This offshore fishery is often referred to as the *haaf* fishery: in other words the deep-sea fishery. The sixareens – six-oared vessels – were some 24ft long in 1774 but a century later they were 35ft. In the early days they were brought in direct from Norway by ship (although some 40ft sixareens are said to have sailed over) because of the lack of timber on treeless Shetland. These came in pieces to be assembled on the islands and cost £6 in the late eighteenth century. By 1830 the locals had begun to import their own timber from Norway and later mainland Scotland and build their own craft. In true Viking fashion they used wide planks of larch, fastened with iron nails, giving the boats that impressive feeling of strength and tradition. What was certain was that it needed this toughness for their venturing into the North Atlantic for sometimes days at a time. They would fish, eat and sleep in the boat that was rigged with a simple squaresail until the lug was adopted. Some say the sixareen is the most tested of British fishing boats because of this ocean sailing and fishing, and that the men themselves were amongst the finest seamen to have lived on these shores. Strong words no doubt, but that they were a special breed of men, willing or not, is for sure. The best place today to learn about the sixareens and other Shetland boats is at the Unst Boat Haven in Unst, the most northerly of the Shetland Isles. The *Far Haaf*, the replica sixareen belonging to Duncan Sandison, is on display there.

LOCHFYNE SKIFF

Dubbed the prettiest of British fishing boats by many people – including me, but I'm a bit biased towards them – the Lochfyne skiffs of Argyllshire and Ayrshire were neither pioneering nor extraordinary in design when the first one was introduced into the Campbeltown in 1884. Developed purely to fish with the ring-net, the first boat was basically a larger version of the earlier trawl skiffs, the main difference being the addition of a cuddy under the foredeck where fishermen could cook and sleep, allowing them to be at sea longer. The introduction of the ring-net had caused upheaval on Loch Fyne. The first experiments were at Tarbert but soon spread, much to the annoyance of the drift-net fishermen who were used to their age-old methods. Within a decade or two the method was banned, it being considered as trawling and destructive to the shoals. During a period of prohibition, as with anything (drinking, drugs, smoking!) there are those that persevere and

thus they worked at night to be undetected. Those that were caught had their boat and nets confiscated. Boats had to become more manoeuvrable to escape detection. When the fishery was eventually legalised in 1867, the use of the ring-net spread quickly so that even those that were opposed to it two decades earlier – presumably the older intransigent fishermen had retired or died – swapped their drift-net for a ring-net. Trawl skiffs were built in place of the earlier wherries. But, as is often the case, it was the introduction of the first larger skiff that brought about a wholesale uptake of the newer design. A trawl skiff had been some 25–30ft whereas the Lochfyne skiff was at least 10ft longer, enabling the sleeping space to be incorporated. They were rigged with a standing lugsail set on a mast, the rake of which was adjustable. In 1908 the first Lochfyne skiff had an engine installed, set over to the starboard side as the net was always handled over the port side, the sternpost not being suited to receiving an aperture. However, in 1922 the first of a new breed of canoe-sterned ring-net boat was introduced which began the decline in the skiffs. Thus, over not much more than a generation, the skiffs came and went as a working boat, one of the shortest lived boats in the fishing industry. Today only a handful have survived.

DRONTHEIM

On the north coast of Ireland Norway yawls (boats probably similar to the square-sailed Lista boats) were being brought by ship because, it has been suggested, the country's timber supplies began to be exhausted in the middle of the eighteenth century. The boats arrived as supplementary cargo and were sold off by the timber-ships as they progressed around the coast. This seems to have been the case throughout the north and west of Scotland. Thus the Norway yawls were then in use throughout this coastline and generally reflected the craft of Gokstad, Norway, Shetland, the Faroes and Iceland. There is a painting by J.W.Campbell in the Ulster Folk & Transport Museum, dated 1822, of Portstewart, County Derry, showing one such yawl, thus supporting the above supposition. The vessel has very curved ends and, at a guess, is about 15-20ft long. There is no sign of any mast or rig. However, we can at least gain a picture of these eighteenth-century vessels in general use around the whole of the West Coast. The Drontheim developed through innovation in the same way as the Shetland sixareen did. Edgar March, in his seminal *Inshore Craft of Britain*, tells us that, in the words of John Smith, boatbuilder, 'many of them came across from Norway [to Shetland] and were improved upon to suit the requirements of the haaf fishermen, being made deeper by the addition of a top strake…the boats from Norway were built with three boards to a side and were very cheap'. In Ireland the builders reduced the sheer, believing the high bow to catch the wind, and used narrower planks to enable local timber stock to be used. Regardless of its origins, the Drontheim was typical of the craft right along the northern coast of Ireland. The Groomsport Yawl, described as 'a whale boat …imported from Norway', carried two dipping lugsails, while the Killough yawl had just one. Skerries yawls were Drontheims in the same way as Greencastle yawls were. These latter boats were used in the Islay fishery where they were referred to as Irish skiffs. These were introduced into the area for the sole reason that Islay was closer to Rathlin Island and

the Irish coast than it was to any harbour of significance on the mainland. A voyage to Campbeltown necessitated navigating around the Mull of Kintyre, infamous for its fog, strong currents and variable, sometimes violent, winds. The result was that boats were bought in from Moville or Portrush and later built on the island to the same design: there is no evidence that the Norway yawls were imported direct to Islay. These skiffs invariably set one spritsail, occasionally two, and when racing, resorted to a standing lug so preferred by the ring-netters in their Lochfyne skiffs. The boats were 26ft in length, although smaller 22ft versions were used when fishing off the Mull of Kintyre. The Campbeltown fishers called these Irish skiffs 'Greenies' after the Greencastle skiff. Records tell of skiffs being brought over by steamer from Ireland and dropped overboard off Sanda Isle to be collected. However, Kintyre, Islay and Colonsay were the geographical limits of the distribution of these craft in Scotland.

ORKNEY AND STROMA YOLES

In Orkney it is the open yoles that stand out as the typical small boat although there are other craft such as the 'whill' which is more or less a smaller version of the yole. Two quite separate yoles – from the North Isles and South Isles

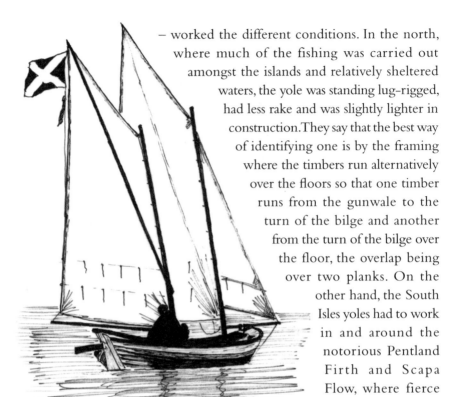

– worked the different conditions. In the north, where much of the fishing was carried out amongst the islands and relatively sheltered waters, the yole was standing lug-rigged, had less rake and was slightly lighter in construction. They say that the best way of identifying one is by the framing where the timbers run alternatively over the floors so that one timber runs from the gunwale to the turn of the bilge and another from the turn of the bilge over the floor, the overlap being over two planks. On the other hand, the South Isles yoles had to work in and around the notorious Pentland Firth and Scapa Flow, where fierce tides run and the seas can be hideous. These were sprit-rigged. The Stroma yole can be said to be a cousin, larger in size and often decked over, unlike the other yoles. They worked almost exclusively in the Firth. Some years ago I met Willie Mowatt MBE and his story is worth mentioning. Although Willie is a blacksmith – the last remaining blacksmith in Orkney – he's also fished for lobsters amongst other things. In reality those of his generation were all rounders, having to work both the land and the sea. To say that Orkney folk are farmers who sometimes fish is an over-simplification but there is a certain amount of truth in it. Willie bought his Stroma yole *Hope* in 1952, primarily to deliver his lobsters over to the mainland. On this particular day he'd sailed over to John O Groats – he calls it Groats – on a perfect day. 'Just like today, it was,' he said, raising a quick eye up towards the bright sun. 'Well,' he continued, 'the wind blew up a bit and so we filled a bit of ballast up.' They'd set off, Willie and three others, and half way across the seven miles that separate South Ronaldsay and Caithness the clouds came on dark and seas built up. The

Pentland Firth is notorious even without wind, when the Atlantic and North Sea tides meet, but given a westerly wind, huge seas build up quickly, catching out many unaware ships. Willie soon realised he'd have to get the sail off and run before it. 'I can still hear that wind today, and I'd never thought I'd witness the foam, like soap suds, and water falling out in lumps.' The boat seemed to tear along the waves as they built up behind. 'Mind,' he said, 'those fellas in the front were too frightened to move although one of them had a camera. The other was back astern with me, pumping at the bilge. I was facing forward. The sound was frightening enough but I had complete confidence in the boat.' They headed east towards the Pentland Skerries that lie almost halfway between Duncansby Head and South Ronaldsay. He'd have gone to Norway if needs be. But they got into the skerries, into Scartan Bay on Muckle Skerry where the surprised lighthouse keepers asked them where'd they come from. Assuming the lifeboat from Longhope would have been sent out to search for them, Willie asked the keepers to get a message through to the coastguards to tell them not to send out the lifeboat. 'I guessed they'd all think that a small boat couldna survive those seas.' The lifeboat was about to launch before the call and the Coastguard informed them that the wind had been logged at over 75mph. 'It was bloody more where we were,' was Willie's reply to that! They stayed on the skerries for two days until the wind veered to the north-west. Fearing it might go north-east which would leave them horribly exposed, he decided to make a run out north-east from the skerries – this entire Scottish coast fears the NE gale – and loop round to the north and then west to miss the worst of the seas. Only when the houses of Grimness were in view did he turn west to get close in under Auld Head and creep back to Burwick to awaiting relatives. The *Hope* proved her worth then according to Willie, and he firmly believes that no other small boat of 23ft in length could have survived such seas. He seems to put this down to Donald Brown whom, he said, built the best boats. According to Willie, Donald Smith was the first builder on Stroma after he moved over from Caithness in the early 1800s. However, this seems disputed as others say it was John Duncan who moved over from South Ronaldsay, although Willie simply says that he was apprenticed to Donald Smith. John Duncan later moved to Herston, to the north of South Ronaldsay and one member of his family eventually moved to Burray where the family yard has only recently ceased work after the retirement of Robin Duncan two years ago. Burray was once an important herring station during the boom of the late 1800s and photographs in the Kirkwall Museum show what is now the slip burdened with barrels of herring and gutting lassies busy at work.

COBLE

The English square-sterned coble has been described as one of the most peculiar and complex beach-based boats working off the coast and was designed and developed over many generations to be launched and recovered stern to shore through the heavy breaking surf of the exposed Northumberland and Yorkshire beaches. Furthermore the coble had to be able to remain at sea for extended periods, sail long distances to the fishing grounds and withstand the notorious North Sea gales. For, unlike similar Cromer crab boats and other beach-based craft of the East Coast, the bigger of the cobles didn't work lobster and crab pots offshore but sailed out into the North Sea to set long-lines. It was the smaller ones that worked the pots. I won't go into the construction of the coble here for it has been covered in many other places, only to say there is no full-length keel but a ram plank. However, I will suggest readers search out a copy of Earnest Dade's North Sea sketchbook entitled *Sail and Oar*, published in 1933, from where this sketch of mine comes.

Not only are the drawings of the cobles and many other types of craft in the North Sea during the 1880s and 1890s, it also shows men at work, the adverse weather and calm summer mornings. There's even a Dutch *bomschuit* on the beach at Scarborough. It's a wonderful evocation of those times, even if the work was harsh and conditions awful. In one picture of Whitby, with all the smokehouses smoking away, he writes of the herring: 'They were smoked at once and made a tasty kipper we knew years ago, very different to what we get now under that name – salt herrings dyed!' My sentiments too, and probably that of Fortune's of Whitby, one of the best smokehouses in the country.

SUFFOLK BEACH PUNT

Another of my favourites, the boat shown here is the *Three Sisters*, IH81, built in Thorpeness for a Mr Ralph in 1896 and bought by maritime historian Robert Simper after he had come across her hull at Orford in 1981. At the time he was looking for a winklebrig but he was attracted to the boat although the owner refused to sell her. He eventually managed to buy her in 1984, at which time the owner relented and sold the engine to him for £120, giving him the boat. It was almost entirely rebuilt by Frank Knights of Woodbridge but now is in great sailing order. I've sailed aboard her on several occasions, sometimes drift-netting for herring off the entrance to the river Deben. These punts were prolific along the Suffolk coast and were used for all manner of fishing including herring and sprats. Smaller punts, such as the Simper-owned *Pet*, another 1902-built boat he has had rebuilt, worked lobster pots. Out of some 350 Suffolk beach punts working along the coast from the river Deben to

Aldeburgh, Dunwich and Southwold, only a handful exist today. Today *Three Sisters* has an engine as well as a full rig. The original punts were all lug-rigged with two masts, the mizzen with its standing lug being stepped against the transom, whilst the main was a dipping lug.

YARMOUTH SHRIMPER

This Yarmouth shrimper *Crangon*, YH55, was once another Simper-owned boat, this time by Robert's son Jonathan. The shrimpers were half-deckers, a tiny cuddy being below the foredeck that extended back to the mast. Again I sailed aboard her, trawling for shrimps in the river. Generally, though, these shrimpers worked out of Yarmouth, catching the brown shrimp in spring and the pink shrimp during the summer, their fishing season being over by October, after which the boats were laid up until the following year. Unlike many shrimping boats, these did not carry a boiler aboard, the catch being landed into Yarmouth and cooked by the fishermen at home and subsequently being sold to the holidaymakers outside their houses. Unlike most of the local punts, the shrimpers adapted a gaff-rig for manoeuvring up and down the river at Yarmouth, especially around the entrance where strong streams could cause havoc. In 1900 there were some sixty-five shrimpers at work, and a few further south at Lowestoft, but by 1931 this fleet had been reduced to thirty-one, most of which had engines fitted. During the Second World War many were requisitioned by the Admiralty to be moored on Oulton Broad to prevent enemy seaplanes from landing. Sadly few survived that dispassionate service so that today only a few, including *Crangon*, have survived. Jonathan sold *Crangon* a few years ago and now she's based between Holland and Germany.

SENNEN COVE CRABBER

The students of the Falmouth Marine School built two replicas of a Sennen Cove crab boat back in 2004 and I recently saw these two boats sailing in the Looe Lugger regatta where they appeared to do pretty well. It has been said that these 20ft luggers were unique, although I'm not sure quite why for aren't most types? That they worked from the Cove that nestles in the coastline of Land's End, amongst some of the wildest parts of the British coastline where huge seas funnel up the Western Approaches, is certain, so they must have had some special sea keeping qualities. However, many other types worked off similarly exposed coasts. What was perhaps an innovation was the addition of wooden shutters that closed off their cut-outs in the gunwale that the oars sat in whilst rowing. A sign of the wild seas having to have a higher freeboard. Cornwall was of course full of small potting boats, those of Cadgwith, Gorran Haven and Port Isaac being recognised as individual types, although I suspect each boat from each beach fishery was slightly different. What I mean here is that they all followed a basic shape that was reflected in the larger mackerel and pilchard boats, and the smaller Mevagissey toshers, all transom-sterned and lug-rigged, although I have to add that some of the boats to the west of the county were double-ended. In 1850 they were eighteen Sennen Cove crabbers that were said to have employed 80 fishermen, although I doubt that each boat had between four and five crew. During the summer season they worked pots as far as the Scillies and seldom ventured far in winter.

ANGLESEY BEACH BOAT

On the beaches of the north and east coast of Anglesey, from Cemaes on the north to Red Wharf Bay on the east coast, the favoured craft were small, transom-sterned open boats of about 20ft in length, although at the end of the nineteenth century a few were built up to 30ft. They were all lug or gaff rigged, although oars were used when chasing the herring shoals that spawned on the sandy seabed of the east coast in the autumn. Most of these boats were built by

Matthew Owen of Menai Bridge whose boatshed still sits above the foreshore there. The only shelter along this coast was either tucked behind the harbour wall at Cemaes or in Amlwch, although the latter was often full of copper ore vessels used for exporting the commodity to South Wales. Moelfre became synonymous with the herring fishery, but long-lining and lobster potting was equally as occupying for the fishermen. The boats themselves were clinker built with a high, dead rise in the bottom plank, enabling the boats to handle well in the strong currents and high winds around the island. In summer, with the growth of tourism on the island in the second half of the nineteenth century, the boats were used for taking trippers around the bay. Herring fishing survived into the 1930s, with the daily 'herring train' supplying the markets of Liverpool and Manchester, but the fishing didn't outlive the war. Further down the coast, on Bardsey Island which lies at the end of the Lleyn peninsular, similar beach boats were built locally, all double-ended.

TENBY LUGGER

Tenby was the all powerful centre, at one time, of the herring fishery in Wales which seems a bit bizarre considering the approaches to the Bristol Channel aren't renowned for herring. Nevertheless, the coast of Pembrokeshire was once teeming with the shoals and Tenby had one of the very first quays in Wales in 1328, funded by Edward III. However, like the herring itself, the centre of the fishery was pretty fickle, so that at other times it was Aberystwyth or Aberdyfi or Nefyn, and in recent times Milford Haven, that landed the most herring. However, Tenby did develop one of the only true Welsh fishing boats of any size, most of the others either being beach boats or English imports. The earliest boats working from the harbour were clinker-built with two masts, each with a small squaresail. In time they adapted to improvements, adopting carvel construction, incorporating a cuddy in the forepeak for shelter and a heavy build to withstand constant grounding in the tidal harbour. With a dipping lug main and small sprit mizzen, these luggers worked lines, drift-nets and oyster dredges. Herring, ironically, became unpopular around the end of the nineteenth century when the shoals deserted Carmarthen Bay. Part of the reason for not wishing to drift for herring lay in the growth of tourism. With bathing machines to operate and tripping boats to take parties out around the bay or ferry folk out to nearby Caldey Island, the visitors gave the fishermen an easy source of income. Fishing, as elsewhere, became an occupation outside of the holiday season, although

there must have been a few fishermen still profiting from the need to supply the restaurants to feed these tourists. As to the luggers, one has survived, albeit in a pretty poor state. Built as the *Three Sisters* by James Newt in 1886, the boat was renamed *Seahorse* at some time and registered as M170 before leaving fishing and ending up languishing under the ownership, I think, of the Swansea Industrial and Maritime Museum, although it might have been the Cardiff Maritime Museum. However, as with many museums, craft such as these get pushed into a shed somewhere and ignored. The Swansea Industrial and Maritime Museum has recently become the Waterfront Museum, a place that in my opinion has managed to destroy the last remnants of any pretence of being a deserved custodian of any boat of importance, the museum being historically bland, far too wide in its scope and almost pathetic in its creed. Which of the museums held it, I cannot confirm, and it isn't really important. What is, though, is that it is both restored and displayed. Recently, I've heard, that the lugger has gone to the West Wales Maritime Heritage Society for restoration and, in the words of Pooh, that can only be a good thing.

ABERDARON LOBSTER BOAT

Albeit a beach boat, the Aberdaron lobster boat is one type that is in a relatively thriving state. In fact, there are more of these clinker-built open boats than any other traditional Welsh fishing boat type and might have survived just because there's no museum nearby! If you go along the coastal footpath heading west and down to Porth Meudy, or Fishermen's Cove, in the summer, you will find a host of these boats either sitting on trailers or racing on a sunny Sunday afternoon. Originally they were small double-ended herring boats that chased the shoals in the autumn, and mackerel in summer. But with the growth of a market for lobsters coinciding with a decline in the drift-net fishery, and a rich supply of the crustaceans hereabout, the fishermen started potting. In time they found they needed a boat with more buoyancy at the after end to row backwards onto a pot, for many boats were capsizing when these were hauled over the pointed stern. Thus they adopted the transom stern with a skeg, and a gaff rig. The majority of the boats originally came from

Aberystwyth until Sion Tomos of Rhiw started building them at the beginning of the twentieth century and continued so up to 1963, after which it was estimated he had built over a hundred of the boats of between 12-16ft. Before him, it is said his father built a few, the oldest surviving *Annie*, said to have been built in 1865, being one of his. Wil Jones of Ty Tanfron was another builder who died before Sion Tomos. Both builders, it is also said, favoured rounded bilges and deep hulls, although the floors are a lot flatter than many of the northern beach boats of Wales. Pwllheli-based Douglas Jones has also built one or two. When I sailed one bright Sunday afternoon, photographing the fleet, some twenty boats were racing and I've read that there are now up to thirty of the fine craft still sailing.

FOUR

WORKING IN DEEPER
WATER UNDER SAIL

INTRODUCTION

As the need for fish grew, and the knowledge of the patterns of the shoals increased, bigger boats were needed to sail further out. At the same time improvements in boatbuilding techniques such as the move to carvel construction and better sail-making skills allowed larger boats to be built at prices the fishermen could afford, although many were built by fishing companies. The change from older hemp nets to cotton nets allowed larger trains of nets to be set in deeper water, and the onset of trawling also produced greater catches that realised higher earnings for bigger boats. Fishing emerged into an industry, with facilities onshore improving distribution throughout the country being made possible by improvements in the infrastructure of, especially, northern Europe. The building of railways was obviously one of the principal motivators in this. Thus fishing became a major employer in coastal communities, with larger ports developing to keep pace with the overall growth in landings.

In the herring fishery, still the major fishery where exports were being made throughout Europe and the British Empire, it is said that up to a quarter of the population were employed in any one place. Wick, in northern Scotland, became the herring capital of Europe with over a thousand boats based there during the spring and early summer season. Later on in the year the boats all moved south, to work off East Anglia. However, trawling was impacting upon herring numbers, with white fish gaining in popularity as herring began to go into decline. On the Atlantic side of France and the Iberian Peninsular, vast fleets of sardine boats were landing huge amounts of the fish which were being canned. Others were sailing westward and northward, coming back with reports of huge amounts of cod. Newfoundland and Iceland were increasingly fished by boats from Spain, France, Britain, Holland and Germany. However, in the Mediterranean, the fishing still remained as it had for centuries – on a smaller scale than in the north although boats were fast spreading their wings and searching for more fishing grounds to feed the populations of the growing towns. Boatbuilding in the Eastern Mediterranean was as old, if not older, than that of the north, and improvements in techniques brought about changes that had hitherto remained the same since the days of Ancient Greece. Europe was changing in many ways and the fishing industry was adapting quickly to suit.

FRENCH *SINAGOT*

Watching a *sinagot* sailing around the bay of Douarnenez several years ago I was struck by just how ancient the boat appeared. Then I discovered that the Romans were said to have built similar boats with iron fastenings as thick as a man's thumb, rigged with hide sails. Centred largely around the Gulf of Morbihan, they were used mostly for oyster dredging rigged with two almost horizontally-peaked lug sails. They were of a basic design, said to have originally been influenced by Scandinavian types, with a long, shallow keel (to work in the gulf), a vertical sternpost and a small cuddy beneath the foredeck. By the end of the nineteenth century they had changed somewhat dramatically, being much bigger in length, the peak of the lugs being much higher and the sternpost having become heavily raked, influences probably brought about through contact with other craft of the coast. By the time of the Great War they were commonplace outside the Gulf in places such as Belle Ile, Quiberon, the small islands of Houat and Hoedic, and inside a line over to Pointe de Croisic, and were mostly fishing shellfish. They remain among the favourites!

LE HAVRE LUGGER

Although registered in the port of Le Havre (H), the smaller fishing stations of Honfleur, Villerville and Trouville had double-ended two-masted luggers working the Bay of Caen, also called the Baie de la Seine, and further out into the English Channel. Worked by three crew and a boy, these vessels fished for herring, sprats and large prawns. In Villerville, which lies between Trouville and Hornfleur, an ancient community of fishers had similar boats that they called *plattes* because, I'm told, of their roundness. The boats, not much larger than 35ft, were quite heavily rigged with two standing lugs, mizzen topsail on a topmast and jib set on a long bowsprit, 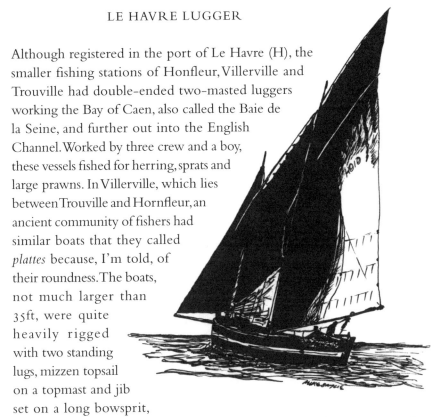 and sported colourful moustaches. Other fishing boats of interest around the bay – and there were plenty of variety of craft – were the lug-rigged *caique d'Yport et Etretat*, the already mentioned *vaquelotte* and the very ancient *picoteux*, a keel-less, flat-bottomed beach boat that, although not really suited to this chapter, is worth a mention purely because of its extraordinary shape.

FRENCH TUNA BOAT

In the Bay of Bourgneuf which lies inside of the island of Noirmoutier, a particular type of 'chaloupe' is said to have only been built at Pornic and Noirmoutier whilst on the banks of the nearby Loire River and at Le Croisic, on the peninsular to the west, other 'chaloupes' were built. Now a 'chaloupe', sometimes called a shallop, refers to the rig of two lugsails with the mizzen mast higher (a bit like a schooner) and usually with a topsail on the mizzen lug. The foremast is situated right up in the eyes of the boat with the mizzen (or main as it's called) amidships, whilst the jib is set on a long bowsprit. What I can't work out is the difference between these two different types of vessels that all seem to be up to some 30ft in length, although the bowsprit alone can be 13ft! Other 'chaloupes' were to be found along the Brittany coast, some fishing the tunny whilst others worked closer inshore. Presumably each had its own local influences that brought about its own unique development.

TRAINERA

The *trainera* is a seine-net boat that appears to have originated in the Basque part of Spain. At some 40ft in length, it was 'chaloupe'-rigged, crewed by up to a dozen men and often rowed at great speed. They became popular vessels all along the northern Spanish coast where seines were operated, and into south-western France. Peniche, on Portugal's west coast, is famous as being where the Spanish *traineras* were first introduced into Portugal. This, in 1913, was to increase the yield of the sardine fishery there, and in turn led to more than a dozen seine-boats being imported that year. The following year one particular boatbuilder of Peniche began building his own version in what became known as the *Vigo type of trainera*. This was a 40ft double-ended galley rigged with one or two dipping lugsails, although lateen sails were later also used. It carried up to fourteen crew and had up to six sweeps either side. Like pilchard seining in Cornwall, these boats set a net around a shoal of sardines. Once they'd detected a shoal using their knowledge of natural appearances (*geitos*) much in the same way as Scottish fishermen searched for herring, they concentrated the shoal by spreading cod roe as bait like the French sardine fishers did (the Spanish used bran). Then the net was cast with a buoy on one end, and the boat rowed around the shoal, pulling the net, until they could join up both ends. Acting like a purse-seine, the net was tightened to entrap the shoal, and then the complete net was rowed into shallow water for emptying into the boats. Sometimes it was pulled ashore and emptied directly onto the beach.

FRENCH SARDINE BOAT

It has been written that, in 1616, the whaleboats of western France were fuller in their shape further forward than aft and that some had been intended as ships' boats. There was a similarity between these and the Spanish *batels* which were the smallest of the *traineras* and had two masts. These whaleboats and seiners were all chaloupe-rigged, and it has been suggested that the characteristic sardine chaloupes of Douarnenez evolved from the earlier boats. What else makes the boats of Douarnenez, the biggest sardine port in France, different is the extreme rake of the sternpost, the roundness of the stern at deck level whilst having a fine exit at the waterline, producing a beautiful form of boat. Both lugs were dipping with the after one being larger than the forward which was in chaloupe style. There were simply hundreds of these boats working from the port and other surrounding harbours. However, when the catches of sardine declined, partly due to mechanisation, smaller boats became popular and single-masted lug-rigged *misainiers* with transoms fished instead. Until about 1900 they were totally open and up to 40ft in length. Transom-sterned variants worked to the south. It has been said that by about 1900 there were over 4,000 boats – both chaloupes and *misainiers* – fishing the sardine and employing 60,000 people, 25,000 of them fishermen.

BARQUE CATALANE

The western side of the Gulf of Lion, in the Mediterranean, was once renowned for its anchovies. From the small harbours of the coast such as Collioure, Roussillon and Banyuls very close to the Spanish border, these lateen-rigged Catalane boats sailed out with five crew and soon became renowned for their speed and seaworthiness. For sure, the boats were common all along the western side of the Gulf, from both sides of the border. In Spain they were referred to as *barca Catalane,* but were nevertheless exactly the same, although flying the Catalane flag. In chapter two we learned about the *llagots*, the canoe-types from Lake Albufeira and these boats are said to have developed from the coastal canoes, but there is some doubt about this. However, there is a degree of similarity between the old *llauts* of the Balearic Islands and the Catalane boats. I once spent a night in Collioure where there was a tangible air of the past even if the last anchovy had long gone from the port. Just seeing the variously decorated anchovy tins in the window of the little French shop was enough. Well, that and the fact that the harbour had several of these brightly painted boats happily tugging at mooring ropes as the twilight descended upon the sweet seascape.

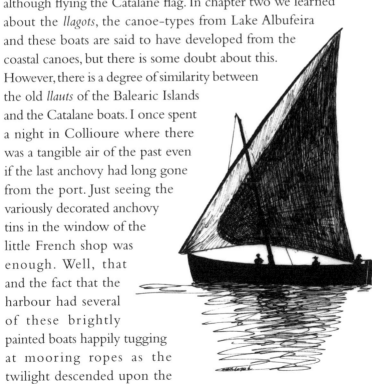

DUTCH LOGGER

It was the French *lougre*, introduced into the Scheveningen fleet in 1865, that so impressed the Dutch fishers. The French boats were powerful luggers developed from three-masted *chasse marees*, famous for terrorising the English fleets during the sixteenth century. The later English luggers materialised from the same design. Over a twenty-year period some 400 *loggers*, as they became known, were built locally, mostly around Rotterdam. The herring fishery here flourished among a keen home market and a healthy German export, with Vlaardingen becoming the major port. With the building of the railways, this hit a peak towards the end of the century and into the twentieth. Steam capstans were introduced into the fleet at the end of the century so that by 1903 nearly all the *loggers* had the advantage of being able to set larger nets. At the same time steam drifters entered service, but this didn't seem to have much effect upon the expansion of the fleets and they continued being built up to the First World War, when Holland retained its neutrality, herring fishing was thriving. The last *logger* was *Dirk*, KW44, which was sold to Germany in 1931 for conversion to a motor sailing coaster. Further east, the first French *lougre* arrived in Germany in 1867 and Vegesack, on the river Weser, became the main base with some fifty *loggers* based their. One survivor is the German *Vegesack*, BV2, built in 1895 by Bremer Vulcan in Bremen. It was restored in 1979, and now sails under the ownership of the society 'Maritime Tradition Vegesack'. Several Dutch *loggers* have also survived, today working as charter vessels.

ESSEX SMACK

The drawing here is actually of a fibreglass Essex smack, one I drew as an illustration for a test-report I once wrote for *Classic Boat*. The Essex smack is the workhorse of the river channels and estuaries of the county, working oyster dredges and beam trawls whilst others spratted. The largest sailed as far as Wales and Holland in search of oysters and whitefish. I'd met the owner of this fibreglass boat as agreed on one of the Norfolk Broads – I can't remember exactly where – and we went for a sail in the new boat, manoeuvring without much difficulty up the waterway and out into a larger lake where I remember getting into a dinghy to take photos and sketch the boat. Taking pen to paper and attempting to draw in a small boat, even in a pretty sheltered sea (or lake), is pretty difficult not just because of the movement of the water but because of the time it takes. By the time you've drawn the deck sheer the boat is a hundred yards away. So he has to tack and make another pass. After a while the owner tends to get fed up so I have to take the resultant drawing home and, with the photographs developed – it was before digital stuff – improve and colour it.

FIFIE

In Scotland, it was the herring fishery that was the champion fishery and the fifie was specifically a herring boat. The shape is said to have come from Dutch influence, the boat having upright stems and sternposts and a powerful rig of two dipping lugs. Before 1850 the boats of the Fife coast were relatively unseaworthy, according to Captain John Washington, RN, who was charged at investigating the fishing boats of Scotland after a particularly nasty storm wrecked numerous herring boats and drowned 100 fishermen. However, he did recognise that those working to the south, around the Firth of Forth, were among the safest, though he attributed this mostly to the skill of the crew. Twenty years after his report the fishermen finally began to see the advantage of decking over their boats whereas previously they had considered this impractical as it hampered the amount of fish they could carry. By 1870 large fifies were appearing up to 70ft in length as they realised the higher earnings it was possible to achieve. Smaller boats, derived from the fifie, worked lines. The smallest were simply fifie yawls whilst those of about 30ft were 'bauldies', the name coming from the Italian patriot Garibaldi who was fighting at the time. The Scots seemed to have a habit of naming their fishing craft after foreign fighters, as we shall see very soon.

SHETLAND HERRING BOAT

Another form of the fifie appeared in Shetland. Because many of the Shetland boats were small open boats, as the herring fishery developed there was a need for much larger vessels and so the fifie, that was already fishing out of Lerwick and other harbours, was found to suit the conditions. At first they retained the two dipping lugs but some were converted to dandy rig – a gaff main and lug mizzen. Many even dropped the mizzen, reverting to a smack rig which was found to be more powerful in confined waters. One such vessel, albeit gaff-rigged, although she was lug-rigged at her launch in 1900, is the *Swan*, LK243, built by Hay & Co. at their Freefield yard in Lerwick. She fished under sail until 1935, after which she had a motor fitted and was later requisitioned for war service until 1945. She continued herring fishing again in season until a seine net winch was installed in 1953. She fished successfully for a few years until being withdrawn in 1956 and languishing for several years, changing hands on several occasions, before arriving in Hartlepool. Her owner there attempted to sail her to Spain twice, aborting because of difficulties. She was then taken to Grimsby where she was bought for £400 in 1974 and a certain amount of restoration work completed, but eight years later came back to Hartlepool and was sold once again. There she languished once again for several years until being bought by the Swan Trust in 1990. They subsequently raised money and restored her back to her original state. She sailed again in 1996 and today sails out of Lerwick, promoting the Shetland fishing heritage and teaching seamanship skills, 'thus keeping alive the techniques of sailing and working a traditional sail fifie'.

ZULU

The Zulu represents the pinnacle of British fishing boat design if you ask me, although I'm sure there will be those that disagree. What cannot be disputed is that they were the perfect machine for catching herring before the advent of steam and petrol/paraffin engines. The name comes from Scottish sympathy for the Zulus of South Africa during the wars of the same name, for the first Zulu appeared around 1879. Many Scots regiments were being killed in a war that was considered an English act of aggravation (again!) and public opinion erred on the side of the natives. The old story is that the Zulu, which was built up to 80ft long, was a crossbreed between the 'scaffie', the favoured fishing boat north of the Moray Firth, and the fifie, as already described. Thus it had the upright stem and a heavily raking sternpost which was typical of the scaffie. Rigged with two massive dipping lugs like the fifie, the boats were renowned for their speed which meant they could get their herring back to market quickly to get the best price. Unfortunately there are no full-sized Zulus surviving today afloat although the 1903-built *Research* sits as an exhibit in the Scottish Fisheries Museum in Anstruther, Fife, whereas a number of smaller half-Zulus (as they've become called) and Zulu skiffs have been restored to sailing order.

MANX NICKEY

We've already seen how William Paynter of St Ives built luggers and how the fishers of the Isle of Man adopted these craft, the reason being they were much more superior to their dandy-rigged smacks. Why call them nickeys? The most plausible answer, which is widely believed, is that the Manx called the Cornishmen 'Nicholas', believing that a vast proportion of the county were Nicholas's! Another reason, though, could have been that the first boat to arrive from Cornwall was the *Nicholas*, although there is no confirmation of this. Whatever the reason, I do like the variety of names of particular types of these boats, and we'll come across a lot more yet. One day maybe someone  will write a complete study of the etymology of these names. With regard to the boats themselves, they were larger than the Cornish counterparts once the Manx started building them on the island. Many were built and it is surprising that none have survived afloat. The only known example is the *Mary Joseph*, N55, built by Paynter in Kilkeel in 1877. She languishes in the ownership of the Ulster Folk and Transport Museum at Holywood, just outside Belfast.

MANX NOBBY

The etymology of the word 'nobby' is just as uncertain. However, the design of this Manx boat came about after the first Clyde 'nabby' arrived to fish in Peel in 1884, hailing from Girvan. This was two years after the first Lochfyne skiff had been built, and the 'nabby' was a variation on the skiff, confined to the eastern side of the Clyde and generally used as a line skiff. One alternative is that the word nabby comes from 'nabbing the fish', although another

possibility is that it is the Scots variation of 'nobby' which has been taken to mean 'smart and elegant, from the trim, stylish appearance'. Furthermore it could refer to the wealth of those – the nobs – owning them! Who knows! What is certain is that they were modelled on the Clyde boats after the nickeys had become too expensive to run. Manx nobbies – not to be confused with Morecambe Bay nobbies which are altogether a different breed of boat – were two-masted, lug-rigged double-enders with a sloping sternpost. Several are still sailing today, including the oldest, the 1901-built *Gladys*, PL61, recently returned from a period of languishment on the west coast of Ireland.

BRIGHTON HOG-BOAT

The drawings of Edward Cooke depicting Brighton around 1830 show squat, dumpy, little clinker-built boats with two masts and leeboards which have been described as Brighton mackerel boats although they also chased herrings and whitefish at times. These were sprit-rigged Brighton 'hoggies' or 'hog-boats', of which there were some seventy based in the growing resort. They were unusual for the time in that many were fully decked and had a forecastle where the fishermen were able to live for short periods, although they never, for some unknown reason, had a stove, so it must have been freezing cold at times. They were very beamy with a 7:4 length to beam ratio which resembled some of the Dutch beach boats. In appearance, they were similar to the lug-rigged beach boats of the opposite French coast. However, by the middle of the nineteenth century the Sussex-style luggers were becoming fully established in the town and were regarded as more handy. Some hog-boats were adapted to compete but were never as successful so that they dwindled in numbers to merely a handful by 1880. The last hog-boat was set alight as part of the 5 November Fawkes celebrations on Brighton beach.

BRIXHAM TRAWLER

The large first-class sailing trawlers of Brixham, Rye and Lowestoft must rate as the most effective English trawlers of the sailing era, probably closely followed by the large Essex smacks. Brixham was the home of the one of the largest fleet of these beam trawlers and even today has not an insignificant fleet of modern beam trawlers based there even if decommissioning is presently reducing this number. The roots of the trawlers stem from the decked boats of the late eighteenth century, seventy-six of which were based in the flourishing port. These were 46ft in length and during the first decades of the next century the boats increased slowly in size so that by mid-century they were over 50ft, and then over 60ft by about 1870. Some 120 boats were working from Brixham then, with another 136 working out Dartmouth,. By this time they had adopted the ketch rig for which they are renowned, although they were called 'big sloops' by the fishermen. Brixham has, over the last decade, gained a fleet of these boats under an umbrella collection and it is thought some 18 vessels still remain intact, some sailing. These include *Leader*, BM156, *Vigilance*, BM76, *Pilgrim*, BM45, and *Provident*, BM28, whilst *Keewaydin*, LT1192 (built in Rye), and *Kenya Jacaranda*, BM57 (ex-*Torbay Lass*), are still around. *Ethel von Brixham*, *Gratitude*, BM9, and *Deodar*, BM313, are in Germany and Sweden, the latter two working from Lowestoft after Brixham. In Lowestoft *Excelsior*, LT472, charters whilst *City of Edinburgh* (ex-William McCann built in Hull) awaits restoration. *Sunbeam* and *Dawn of the Day*, LT565, are other Lowestoft boats, also in Scandinavia. Their legacy is ensured for now.

THAMES BAWLEY

The word 'bawley' probably is a derivative of 'boiler' for these boats are the shrimp boats of the Thames, although they went whelking outside of the shrimp season. They developed from the earlier Peter boats, the original fishing boats of the river. It has been suggested that these were originally built to transport the congregation of St Peter's Cathedral from across the river, hence the name, and that they worked Peter nets which are deemed to be seine nets. Documented evidence from the sixteenth century states that they were 12ft rowing boats but, as they desired to venture further down river, they built bigger boats with a small spritsail. They even had a small wet-well, one of the first European fishing craft to do so. Originally double-enders, they adopted the transom, some having forecastles with accommodation. But by 1840 the bigger smack-rigged bawley had gained favour and the Peter boats faded from popularity. The bawley has a long straight keel, transom with little rake, high freeboard and initially little sheer until this became more pronounced at the bow. The short mast sets a loose footed gaff sail on long gaff boom so that the leech is almost vertical. A topsail is set on a very long topmast and the foresails are set on a long bowsprit. I use the present tense because, although there were once 100 bawleys working out of Leigh-on-Sea alone as well as many from other parts of the estuary, there are several still sailing.

GUIDE ME, FY233

This Cornish lugger is well known in lugger circles because of its tendency to win regattas, although this must partly be due to the skill of her owners Jono and Judy Brickhill. She was built in 1911 in Looe and worked from there until 1967, after which she briefly worked as a crabber out of Guernsey. In the 1970s she was bought by her present owners and brought back to Cornwall and underwent restoration. Afterwards they sailed the boat, still engineless, to South Africa, South America and the Caribbean before bringing her back to Gweek, her present home. She's a normal visitor to maritime festivals and local regattas, and it's a pretty sight watching the vessel being rowed up the Looe River to moor alongside the other, largely engined, luggers tied up against the quay of West Looe, the applause from the other boats echoing around the harbour. She's traditionally rigged with dipping lugs and a foresail set on a bowsprit – something that the luggers from west Cornwall never had.

CHILDREN'S FRIEND

Children's Friend, although rigged today as a west Cornish lugger, is not Cornish in any other way and was in fact built by Weatherhead of Cockenzie in Scotland in 1938 as a seine-netter under the name *Sunbeam III* and registered as LH215. She was owned by the Neil family and worked out of Port Seton. She later moved to the West Coast of England, being renamed as *Children's Friend* and registered as FD225 before ending up fishing out of Newlyn for several years and subsequently being threatened with decommissioning, and the ensuing scrapping that would inevitably occur. She was then bought by Billy Stevenson and rigged as a Mount's Bay lugger with the wheelhouse being removed. Although built as a motor fishing boat, she's included here to show that it is possible to take a vessel from another part of the country and transplant her elsewhere, rather than purely as an example of a Mount's Bay lugger. That the same influences impacted upon the fishermen and their boats even though there was little contact shows that designs were developed to suit localities rather than any idea of national boundaries. Thus Cornish boats were influenced by the French and the Scots by the Scandinavians and Dutch. Nevertheless the result was often similar.

YARMOUTH LUGGER

The great three-masted luggers were in all reality, excepting the herring busses and cod smacks, both of which were in actuality fishing bases for smaller boats, the first deep-sea fishing boats of the English Channel and North Sea. These boats developed from earlier square-sailed craft in latter part of the eighteenth century and were extremely bluff-looking clinker-built craft of up to 60ft in length. Yorkshire, the South Coast and Cornwall all had their own luggers, each with its own type of hull. In the early nineteenth century the men of Yarmouth – home to the Great Autumn Herring Fishery – were amongst the first to drop one mast, there being over a thousand two-masted luggers there in 1896. These two-masted boats would drop the main mast, lowering it into a crutch, when lying to their drift-nets, normally at night when the herring come to the surface to feed off the plankton. Similar luggers were to be found all along the Norfolk and Suffolk coasts, and with most registered in Yarmouth at the time, many of these would be included in the thousand mentioned.

Above: The Manx nobby
Gladys sailing in 2007.

Right: The Scottish fishing
boat *Ocean Pearl* in 2007.

Mary Colette, a replica of a typical lobster boat from south-west Ireland.

Above: Two Galway hookers racing at Kinvara, 2007.

Opposite top: Replica of an eighteenth-century 'chaloupe' from Brittany.

Opposite centre: The Danish 'kotter' *Dente Dorte*.

Opposite bottom: Nebuleuse, a tunny boat from Camaret.

A typical 'langoustier' from north-west France.

The Norwegian cutter *Faxsen*, built in 1916.

Danish fishing boat *Tina Husted*.

Above: The replica 'bisquine' *Cancalaise*, built in 1987.

Left: The replica sinagot *Crialeis*, built in 1990.

Opposite above: General Leclerc, a scallop boat from the Rade de Brest, dating from 1948.

Opposite below: Though not a fishing boat, this is *Agnes*, a replica Scillonian pilot cutter, similar to many that probably fished.

The Danish kotter *Lola*, built in 1919.

Vieux Copain, a 1940-built tunnyman with the traditional Dundee rig.

Cornish lugger *Snowdrop*.

Reder Mor, a 1992-built replica of a traditional Breton coastal fishing boat.

Above: A southern French coast fishing boat, *c.*1900.

Opposite top: The German herring 'logger' *Vegesack*.

Opposite centre: The basque 'chaloupe' *Brokoa*, built in 1991 and typical of a Biscay seiner.

Opposite bottom: The half-zulu *Leenan Head*, built in Scotland for the Irish fisheries, now owned in Brittany.

Above left: Two typical Greek fishing boats at Skiathos in 2003.

Above right: The Brixham trawler *Pilgrim*. (Photo Bill Wakeham)

Three typical inshore Greek *trechandiri* peaceful at anchor.

FIVE

THE ADVENT
OF STEAM

INTRODUCTION

Although the first steam vessels had been chugging along inland waterways since the late eighteenth century and Henry Bell's *Comet* had first sailed on the Clyde in 1812, steam power first entered the fishing industry in the 1850s, a time when the Industrial Revolution was at its height, transforming Britain, its powerhouse, and spreading throughout Europe. At the time smacks and luggers were being towed in and out of their harbours by steam-powered paddle tugs. Ten years later the same tugs were towing smacks around out at their fishing grounds and thus the idea of fishing under steam arose. A pioneering boat – the *Thistle* – was launched in Dartmouth in 1868, followed by *Florence* the next year. But these boats were wooden and too small to be effective and larger ones were needed. In the north William Purdy from North Shields in Northumberland was trying to trawl a net from his tug in 1877 and his tug *Messenger* produced good results on his second trip out. The fishermen around him, meanwhile, looked on incredulously as if thinking 'what the hell is this fool up to?'! But with each improvement in boat technology, fishermen have often regarded these changes as crazy and, although very slow on the uptake, have eventually seen sense and, more importantly, increased profits, and copied. The first purpose-built iron steam trawler with the characteristic hull they became renowned for, appears to have been the *Zodiac*, built in 1881 for the Great Grimsby Steam Trawling Co. The boat's catches were four times that of the smacks although she burned four tons of coal a day. Because she could steam at nine knots she was always the first home and her profits were much greater than any of the sailing boats.

However, safety aboard the vessels seems never to have played a major part in their concerns. Fishing was then the most dangerous of occupations and it always had been. Even with such industries as mining and quarrying where men were often killed, it was still fishing that had the worst statistics for fatalities.

Fishing remains to this day still the most dangerous of occupations with three men, on average, killed each month in Britain. That's not to say safety wasn't improved upon the steamers that soon started to be built as the floodgates opened. By the late 1880s there were hundreds of steam trawlers built. In Scotland the first purpose-built steam trawler appeared a year later than in England. Soon these boats were working all round the coast of Britain – from Aberdeen and Lowestoft to Milford Haven and Fleetwood.

It was the same in the rest of Europe. In Germany, Bremenhaven became the main steam port with over 200 vessels working from there. In Belgium, steam first arrived in 1884 in the form of the *Prima* at Oostende. The following year saw the second steam trawler *Elisabeth*. So began the decline in the sailing boats. It was the same in the northern French ports where steam trawlers were first introduced into the country. In the south-west, Portugal got its first steam seiner – called a 'fire' seiner – in the closing years of the century whilst Spain had to wait another twenty years before the first steam-seiner arrived from the French port of St Jean de Luz.

Steam drifters, on the other hand, were slow on the uptake as fishermen believed the sounds of the engine scared the fish away, as well as the propeller being a danger to the net. The first successful steam drifter was the Lowestoft-built *Consolation* in 1897 although experiments on Scottish drifters had already taken place and some built which were disasters. By 1913, though, there were 1,800 steam drifters which were different to the trawlers in that the accommodation was aft, the freeboard low and they had low counter sterns. During the First World War some 1,502 steam drifters and 1,467 steam trawlers were requisitioned for war service by the British Admiralty and 376 of these were lost at sea. Some fished throughout the war and continued afterwards. However, by then the motorised fishing boat had appeared and the days of steam-powered fishing boats were soon over. Only a handful remain in Europe.

EARLY STEAM BOAT

The *Waterwitch*, LH961, is regarded as one of Scotland's first successful steam drifters, built in 1880 in Leith for John Mackenzie, a fish curer from Wick,

according to Iain Sutherland in *The Fishing Industry of Caithness*. Although Mackenzie's earlier steamer *George Lock* was launched in 1869 in Wick, she was not considered very effective and Mackenzie converted her back to sail the following year as the engine was constantly giving trouble. At the time all the steamboats were basically wooden sail boats under full rig with an engine added. *Waterwitch* caught 300 crans of herring in her first year but she hadn't been as profitable as the sailing boats. She was sold to the Irish Fisheries protection services where she worked for several more years.

LYDIA EVA, YH89

The 1930-built steam drifter *Lydia Eva* is one of a very few of these superb-looking craft still around and she recently won a Heritage Lottery grant

to be restored so is well worth a mention here. Built for fisherman Harry Eastick to replace three earlier vessels (*Harry & Leonard*, *Young Ernie* and *H.F.E.*), she was ordered from the King's Lynn Slipway Co. and originally intended to fish in the prolific fishing grounds off the Norwegian coast. However, Eastick considered her to be too bluff in the bow for working these exposed grounds, the heavy swell, he believed, would ruin his drift nets. Thus he added 60 tons of ballast and her first trip was round to Castlebay in the Outer Hebrides where, in July 1930, she fished for seven weeks and earned £3,000, a massive amount of money then. She returned to her home port of Yarmouth where she made another £3,000 over the winter. Once she has been restored, she will again be on display at, alternatively, Lowestoft and Yarmouth, where visitors are welcome aboard.

EARLY STEAM *TRAINERA*

This steam *trainera* was typical of the type in use along the western seaboard of Portugal after they were introduced into the fleets in the closing years of the nineteenth century. Built of wood, these boats had the high funnel which steam fishing boats from all over Europe are renowned for. The hull shape is not unlike the first British purpose-built craft, said to have been modelled on a typical English smack, but with a more characteristic Portuguese counter stern. The shape of the later motorised craft from this coast closely resembles this steamer.

BELGIUM STEAMER

As we've seen, steam trawlers and later drifters were adopted by fishermen from most of the north European countries in the 1880s. Belgium was no exception and this boat worked out of Oostende up to the First World War.

STEAM DRIFTER

Although there is something so complete and solid about these vessels, it's hard to explain exactly what I mean. What is also surprising is the numbers of them that were built. In Europe we are talking possibly of over 5,000 vessels over fifty years or so. The other day I was reading *Steam Drifters Recalled – Portgordon to Portsoy* (by Alexander Buchan *et al*) – the book is one of a series on steamers – and I was amazed at the number of yards listed as building these steam drifters, 140 of them, most being on the East Coast of England and Scotland, as well as a few in Holland, France and even Canada. Many of the yards listed probably only built one or two boats whilst others, such as the well known John Chambers (later Chambers & Colby) built many. From this sketch you will understand why the fishermen had two nicknames for their boats, the first being 'Pipestalkies'. To understand the second, you might have to be a smoker, for it was named after the well-known cigarette, 'Woodbines'! Like the cigarette, it provided a lot of smoke!

SIX

EARLY MOTORISED CRAFT

INTRODUCTION

The first instance of a paraffin motor being fitted into a fishing boat occurred in Denmark in 1895 and five years later on an Esbjerg's smack's *snurrevodjolle* (the small boat working the seine net before it was hauled aboard) had an engine from Mollerup of Esbjerg fitted. However, in the closing stages of that century the idea never really caught on. The first purpose-built British boat to have an engine installed was built by Henry Reynolds at his yard at Oulton Broad, Lowestoft in 1901 at a cost of £1,600. This, the *Pioneer*, LT368, was built on smack lines with the normal rig but with space made available for a 38hp 4-cylinder Globe Marine Gasoline engine from Philadelphia, USA, that itself cost £680. *Pioneer* had some startling earnings. Four years later another *Pioneer*, ML30, was built in Anstruther on fifie lines with a 25hp single-cylinder Dan engine fitted. Others quickly appeared, such as the Sheringham whelk boat *Reaper*, YH34, that had a Gardner paraffin motor fitted. In Ireland J. Tyrrell & Sons Ltd of Arklow launched the *Ovoca* in 1908 for the Fisheries Department of the Board of Agriculture for Ireland, in which a 20hp Dan motor was installed. However, the vessel had been designed by Jack Tyrrell in 1905 and today is considered as the very first purpose-built motor fishing vessel in Britain with a cruiser stern. However, as well as building new boats with motors, a number of sailing boats had motors installed. On the west coast of Scotland the Lochfyne skiff *Brothers*, CN97, was the first to have a Kelvin 7.9hp unit. Another Lochfyne skiff *Lady Carrick Buchanan*, CN38, was another motorised later that year with a 7½hp Thornycroft paraffin unit.

And so the advent of motorisation had arrived and boats were quickly converted even if the fishermen were again doubtful at first. Some boats suited having propeller shafts fitted in the sternpost, part of the rudder being cut away to form an aperture, whilst others didn't. By 1919 there were 9,124 fishing boats working in Scotland alone. Of those 324 were steam trawlers, 872 steam drifters, 1,844 were motorised and 4,058 were sailing craft, albeit mainly of the small variety, many of which were never converted and the remaining being small open boats. In northern Europe the story was the same with a flood of conversions and new builds. In the Mediterranean it was another decade before motorisation affected the fishing fleets but once it happened, it was unstoppable. In Scotland, though, motorisation had brought about another change in hull shape as the new breed of ring-net boat arrived in Campbeltown in 1922. On the east coast the motorised fifie arrived followed soon after by the motorised herring drifter. The typical Scottish MFV had arrived, spurred on after the building of *Cutty Sark* in 1928 with a cruiser stern, influenced by those from Denmark and, perhaps, Ireland. In Scandinavia a similar pattern lead to the cruiser-sterned seine-net boat that were so prolific later on in the twentieth century.

Some of craft shown in this chapter are types that evolved after the advent of motorisation and are not vessels that simply had motors fitted to existing boats although, as in the case of the Cornish lugger and *Glad Tidings III*, these are boats that have been converted into motorised fishing vessels.

DANISH SHARK-CUTTER

In Frederikshaven, in the north of Denmark, motor-seiners, smacks working Danish seine nets or *snurrevod* (see above) that worked in deep water, started having motors fitted. Many of the smacks had come from Britain after they were sold off with the advent of steam trawlers and most were counter-sterned. The units were small so that the rig was retained although the power was increased to 14hp by 1910. These boats became known as *haj-cutters* or shark-cutters by those still working under sail. Also by 1910 the same boats were working out of Esbjerg on the west side of the country and most were counter-sterned as well as having wet-wells. However, by 1930, the cruiser stern had become regarded as more suitable in hulls in which the power of the motor was fast increasing and with increasing ice facilities, the wet-well gradually disappeared. Many of the shark-cutters built in the 1930s have survived and some are sailing today in Britain where they are termed 'Danish kotters'.

FRASERBURGH YOLE

Nobles of Fraserburgh developed a range of small motorised yoles, based on earlier sailing yoles. These were all about 25ft in length, double-ended and retained a rig of a dipping lugsail and most had Kelvin engines fitted. They proved an adaptable boat for inshore fishing and fifty worked from the harbour at any one time. J. & G. Forbes and Tommy Summer also built a few with the last one being built in 1942. Several remain, *Cariad* being seen in Fraserburgh harbour, moored alongside a couple of others, in about 1999. Today *Progress* has been restored and is moored on the river Lyner, Cornwall whilst *Shepherd Boy*, FR423, built by Nobles in 1934, and fishing from Fraserburgh, Whinnyfold, Cruden Bay and Broughty Ferry before moving to North Wales, was about to be restored until the owner gave up. Until a couple of years ago her shell lay alongside the road in east Anglesey.

VERONICA

Veronica was built in 1934 by Weatherhead of Cockenzie for the Sloan Brothers of Ayrshire, renowned ring-net fishermen. When she first started fishing the ring-net under the registration BA46, she neighboured (ring-net boats always worked in pairs through the very nature of the method and it was always said that the two boats 'neighboured' each other) *Virginia*, BA66, until the latter was replaced with another *Virginia*, BA202, both of which were also built at Cockenzie. Weatherhead ring-netters were regarded amongst the best of the boats although James N. Miller of St Monans, Fife, Walter Reekie of Anstruther and St Monans, Fife and James Noble of Fraserburgh were also renowned builders of these craft. All were characterised by the lovely sweep of their canoe stern, low freeboard and the builder's particular symbolic stem. Alexander Noble began building ringers (as they became called) from 1946 at Girvan and his boats were favoured by the Clyde men. *Veronica*, however, was sold to Port Seton and worked the seine net as LH45 until 1975, at which time she was de-registered and converted to a yacht, the work started at the Weatherhead yard she had been built at. However, with fishing boat building in the Doldrums, the yard was forced into receivership and *Veronica* moved to Glasson Dock to be finished. She was eventually completed by 1985 and sold in 1994, after which she became a charter boat on the west coast of Scotland until being sold again and taken to the South Coast where, I believe, she is based on the Isle of Wight.

GLAD TIDINGS III

This boat came from the east coast of Scotland in 1922 and appears to be a small 'scaffie' type of 40ft in length with a sloping sternpost and she was owned by the Blair family whilst in Campbeltown, registered as CN202 and ring-netted under power. According to Angus Martin in *Fish and Fisherfolk* (House of Lochar, 2004) she was previously registered as INS162 and came from Avoch on the north coast of the Moray Firth. Robert Ross is quoted in the book as recalling her to have a rounded stem 'for sailin' over the drift nets in the Inverness Firth'. That description of her shallow forefoot would suggest she was indeed a 'scaffie' type. In the summer of 1996 I travelled up to Cromarty Firth to take the lines off a boat called *Wisp*. Although her lineage was unknown, it was discovered that she had acted as a ferryboat between Meikle Ferry and Skibo on the Dornoch Firth. Deciding to call her a Moray Firth yawl for no other reason than we didn't know what else to, I took off the lines and drew her up. Her sternpost raked at a much more extreme angle than *Glad Tidings* although there are many other similarities. *Wisp*'s owner thought she had been built at Nairn and was over a hundred years old although I discovered references to such boats being based at Avoch. *Wisp* was only 32ft long, 8ft shorter than *Glad Tidings*. However, they made a useful comparison even if we still do not know the exact ancestry of both boats and, in all probability, never will.

MOTORISED CORNISH LUGGER

We've already come across a couple of Cornish luggers but this is a double-ended one from St Ives, built as a sailing boat but converted to a motorised lugger. The Cornish fishermen used to install their engines in the forward part of the boat with a long shaft leading right back to the sternpost. According to Paul Greenwood in his autobiography of the time he was fishing out of Looe (*Once Aboard a Cornish Lugger*, Polperro Heritage Press, 2007) the boat he worked upon, the *Iris*, FY 357, had three engines, all Listers, with 45hp in the aft cabin and 30hp and 21hp in the forepeak. When they were steaming they used all three engines but when working their gear only the after one was fired up. All three propellers emerged on the port quarter keeping them clear of the nets worked on the starboard side. The lugger shown here also had its propellers on the port side, although I can't remember exactly how many there were. Three, I think.

BONNIE LASS

I've always liked the shape of the small inshore creel boats of the Scottish coast, most of which were to be found between the Firth of Forth and Montrose. The *Bonnie Lass* I used to see every day when I was in St Andrews, living in my van alongside the harbour for several months. She was a Millers of St Monans boat, officially termed a Fifer creel boat, was built in 1962 and registered as KY293. She was for sale at the time for a considerable sum (I can't remember how much but thought it a bit excessive) but nevertheless she sold and I believe the present owner is thinking about selling her again. In 2001 I helped students at the Scottish Institute of Maritime Studies based at the university there take the lines off her. I myself took the lines off several other creel boats including the Millers-built *Quest IV*, ME70, which I found on the beach at Gourdon, and *Comely*, KY175, another creel boat built by Smith & Hutton of Anstruther in 1957. The yard of Smith & Hutton is today part of the Scottish Fisheries Museum. All boats were between 22ft 5in and 26ft, the Millers' boats having a shorter keel of 18-19ft whereas the *Comely*'s keel was 24ft, the boat hardly having any rake in the sternpost and stem. This just shows how two yards, only several miles apart, can build similarly worked boats to a different design.

PETERHEAD YOLE PD381

All along the east coast of Scotland there are today the remnants of boats built in the early stages of motorisation. This one, registered in Peterhead, I found on the hard at Boddam. Built on the traditional fifie lines of upright stem and sternpost, it looks like the sternpost has been cut away to make room for the propeller aperture. There's nothing standard about these vessels as each builder built to his own eye, perhaps adapting if the owner wanted some improvement. They are all under 30ft and of various shapes so that to classify them is impossible and pointless. They are numerous and built for purpose – the creed of working boats!

SEVEN

THE DEVELOPMENT OF MOTORISED CRAFT

INTRODUCTION

There is a whole pile of nostalgia about the end of what has been coined the 'sail and oar age', and, whilst I can understand it and feel a good amount of sentiment towards the vessels myself otherwise I wouldn't be writing this book, it has to be said that motorisation did make life a hell of a lot easier for those at sea. I think that is too often overlooked these days when considering the past, perhaps because the idea of living without the internal combustion engine is completely beyond our capability now that it is so much a part of our lives. We, as a society and not as individuals, have become immune to alternatives even if we do feel we desire them. As diesel engine technology advanced in reliability and efficiency during the 1930s and '40s, the fishermen too put more faith in them, and it's fair to say that new boats refrained from having an auxiliary rig. Scottish boatbuilding advanced considerably, prompted by the war and the need for naval vessels to protect the country from Nazi Germany's threat of invasion and U-boat attack. Once hostilities had ended in 1945, fishing began once again in earnest for the population was in dire need of food, rationing continuing into the 1950s. New boats were built with government help in the funding. It was a time of prosperity in the fishing industry for most boats.

GERMAN *KRABBENKUTTER*

'Krabben' are not what you think – they're shrimps, from the healthy fishery in the shallow waters all along the north-west German coast. Four centuries

ago herring was king here. Taxes were paid on fish landed on the island of Sylt, at Germany's extremity along its northern border with Denmark, and where the epicentre of this herring fishery was to be found. In 1500 there were some 220 rowing boats from the island fishing within sight of Helgoland, that tax-free haven some thirty miles offshore. Twenty years later this had increased to 340 boats. This, remember, was at the time that the German Hanseatic merchants controlled the fishery of Sweden's south-west coast. No doubt they brought influence to bear upon these fishers. But, by 1607, the buss fishery had established itself. These busses had a crew of forty-five men and there were some fourteen ships engaged. However, these have been referred to as 'large ewers', a description the accuracy of which I doubt. Four years later only four had survived, with small, open boats – 'fischer-jolles' – in control. A century on and these small 'jolles' had acquired a square-sail, and, by 1771, there were thirty such craft working out of Sylt. In the next century, the kutter was adopted, much as the English smack was introduced on the river Elbe, and this seems to have coincided with the re-emergence of the shrimp fishery. Maybe one supplanted the other. The water about the islands between the mouth of the Elbe and Sylt are shallow, and perfect breeding grounds for the shrimp. These craft, influenced by the Danish cutters from the north, became known as the *krabbenkutters* or 'shrimp cutters'. They were single-masted gaff cutters of up to 10m in length, and were built at harbours such as Tonning and Busum. After motorisation, the first one being engined in 1906, these cutters were easily adapted and, although their shape altered somewhat in fullness, they retained a certain similarity to before. The local yard at Tonning built some 190 motorised cutters between 1920 and 1959, when the last one was built. This was the *Pornstrom*, TON4, which today sits ashore as a silent reminder of the hundreds of these craft that were built. Several sailing cutters remain afloat today. Today shrimpers work out of Tonning, Busum and Friederickskoog, but of course these are modern boats that bear no resemblance to these cutters.

ARCACHON OYSTER BOAT

In the Bassin d'Arcachon on France's southern Biscay coast, the *pinassottes* or *espinasses* were single-masted dipping-lug sailed craft, very narrow with curved pointed ends and used to carry oyster spat back from the breeding grounds to the sheds on shore. They were lightly built, renowned for their

good turn of speed, and had two or three rowing points, depending on the size of the boat. The mast was set about one quarter of the boat's length from the bow. In 1727 they were documented as being 14ft long with one sail. In the early part of the twentieth century the fishermen fiercely contested regattas each year, but once motorisation arrived after the first world war, this all changed. The shape of the hull of what became known as the *pinasse* was altered slightly, with a more prominent upwards tuck to the bow sheer line and increase in fullness. Size, too, increased to between ten and fourteen metres. Short fore and after decks were built in, with narrow side decks, a cabin about amidships and a hold forward of this to hold the oysters. This area had removable covers, perhaps to allow more oysters to be stowed above the hold. Several of these pinasses remain moored up about the creeks, while more stand ashore. Some are still used for fishing and others for pleasure. However, as regards the oyster-culture, they are largely redundant nowadays because in the 1960s another type craft, what can only be termed a barge, was adopted, this being easier to manoeuvre and capable of carrying a heavier load. These are flat-bottomed, single-engined, barges which only have a few inches of draught, an advantage leading to less hanging about on the sand banks waiting for the tide to drop. The design has hardly changed today and appears to be normal in other areas of the French oyster trade.

GREEK *TRECHANDIRI*

The *trechandiri* is the workhorse of Greek coastal fishers, as well as being used these days to ferry holidaymakers to beaches inaccessible by road. Throughout Greece there are literally dozens of tiny yards where wooden *trechandiria* are being built, always from pine, from Samos if possible, and, like most of the Mediterranean boats, are colourfully painted, as anyone having visited Greece will attest. They adorn the picture postcards seen on every street corner. White hulls, brightly painted superstructures, yellow fishing nets with red floats and vivid reflections in the turquoise sea is what comes to mind at the mere mention of a Greek harbour. In the harbours of Crete, Ios, Santorini, Kos, and other islands I've stood and watched as they've sailed in with their day's catch. Once, whilst visiting Kalimnos, famous for its sponges, I'd sailed to an overnight stay at Pserimos aboard such a vessel. Today fitted with modern diesels, these craft have remained largely the same ever since they were introduced. The advent of motors in the 1920s simply

ΨΑΡΟΒΑΡΚΑ
(FISHING BOATS)

The 'TRECHANDIRI'
OF
GREECE

produced a fatter, fuller body section, whilst in profile they were unchanged. Once the rig was removed superstructures were added! They are ubiquitous throughout the Aegean – that sea of thousands of islands – and have one thing in common, a length/beam/depth ratio of round about 9:3:1. There are two schools of thought on their origins. Some say they developed from a particular type of *caique*, first built in Hydra in 1658, while others suggest they evolved from the *trabaccolo*, a type of sailing vessel used for trading in the Adriatic. A *caique*, though, is not a specific type of Greek fishing boat. It is a generic term for a vessel used for trading, and can also be used to include professional fishing craft. They are normally anywhere between 15 and 200 tons. Thus vessels such as the *perama* and *karavoskara* are called *caiques*. *Trechandiria* have a relatively shallow draught for working close inshore, have a good carrying capacity, are fast, and are renowned for being one of the most seaworthy of Greek craft. They were first used both for trading and fishing, the former being the larger at up to 40 tons. These were rigged with two masts with lugsails, this arrangement being called *psatha,* the after lug being extremely high-peaked. Smaller fishing versions had only one mast setting a *sakkoleva* or type of spritsail. Prior to this, lateen sails were common, although the *sakkoleva* was deemed more suitable for rough seas. The *psatha* could drive a vessel closer to the wind yet needed more crew.

MALTESE *LUZZU*

The internal combustion engine was introduced into Malta – like much of the Mediterranean – in the 1920s, and the *ferilla* was found unsuitable because of her sharpness. The *luzzu* was introduced from Sicily as a form of the *gozzo.* The flatter shape of these boats allowed engines to be fitted. They were larger than the older boats as well, up to 40ft, and much heavier and higher in the water, but that those that were built on the island were developments of the *ferilla* was obvious from a visual point of view. Engines were unreliable at first so the single sprit was retained although they were still rowed at times. Today, though, it's a different picture as those that are

still working have up to four engines. With one central engine and two in the wings and the fourth acting as a generator, there's no fear of needing a sail. The *luzzu* drawn here I saw several years ago whilst on holiday in Malta. The *arznella* she's carrying is a large creel set in 20-30 fathoms of water in winter, with herring as bait, to catch 'picarel', a pelagic fish similar to pilchards. However, the boats are still decorated in bright colours which they believe attract the fish and have the Eye of Osiris fixed either side of the prow to keep the evil spirits away. With Malta having just joined the European Union, let's hope those eyes keep the evil bureaucrats of Brussels away!

TUNISIAN BEACH BOAT

I saw this boat on the beach in Hammamet, Tunisia, and decided to include it because it was very similar to the beach boats still working the southern coast of Spain and parts of the West Coast of Italy. A ubiquitous type of small motorised open double-enders that work nets within a few miles of the shore. I remember photographing the boats on the beach at La Linea, across the border from Gibraltar and there was very little difference.

MOTOR FIFIE

These motorised craft – also called super-bauldies – were the next stage of developement in the 1940s and '50s. Built mainly for seine-net fishing, they were based on the early fifies, or the smaller bauldies as the name suggests. There's also an argument that they were a cross between the fifies and Zulus, with a sternpost that sloped a little. However, as a Zulu was a hybrid itself, this suggestion seems a bit silly. Again, this is an example of development in design purely from usage and discussion between builder and owner and emphasizes the impossibility of classifying each boat into a particular group.

LILY

I drew a picture of *Lily* in 1996 purely because she was one boat still on the fishing register at that time, yet that had been built before 1950. This was for an article on the subject in *Fishing Boats* and the photo had come from Mike Craine who had seen her in Greenock. Although registered at Ballantrae, she was working out of the Clyde port at the time, trawling in the upper reaches of the Firth. I thought her quite pretty from the photograph, although she looks like she has been raised up. She was built in Arnside in 1941 where many of the Morecambe Bay nobbies came from the renowned Crossfield family of boatbuilders. *Lily* looks a bit 'nobbyish' in the stem if you take into account she's 'rose-on', but with a transom stern she's completely different aft.

BRAW LADS

Braw Lads is an Eyemouth-built boat from the Weatherhead yard. She was launched in 1955 as a seine-netter and registered BK20, but, because she was underpowered, she wasn't very successful at seine netting so spent time at the creels instead. She was eventually sold to Cornwall where she fished under the registration FH20 until leaving fishing in 1996 after being sold to John Habgood. However, I include her for another reason – to clarify the Weatherhead boatbuilding yards. Alexander Weatherhead started building boats in Cockenzie from half-models and his son William John continued after him. Cousin William then started in Eyemouth but the Cockenzie yard went into liquidation and was bought by J. Samuel White. A few years after William John opened a yard in Port Seton with John Blackie and together they traded as Weatherhead & Blackie between about 1958 and 1965. They moved to Dunbar because of better facilities and also built steel boats for a while at Berwick.

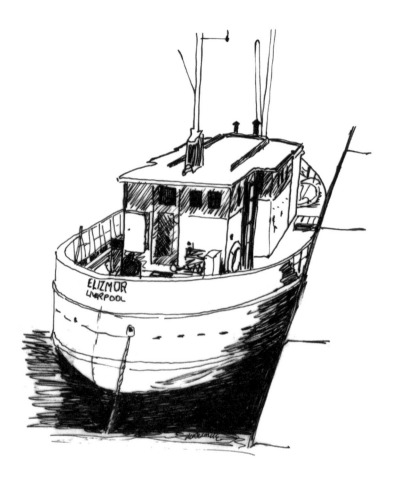

ELIZMOR

Elizmor is a Millers of St Monans boat built in 1948 on their traditional 54ft ring-netter lines. She was delivered to skipper Edward McEwan of Maidens and registered as BA343. At the ring-net she neighboured *Arctic Moon*, BA369, another Millers boat and together these boats followed the herring shoals around the west coast of Scotland, the Isle of Man and Southern Ireland, although the boats had to convert to Irish registry for the latter. Returning to Girvan in 1959, the boats were rigged for dual-purpose fishing, prawn trawling and ring-netting, although soon *Elizmor* had become a full-time trawler. Subsequently, with *Silver Lining*, BA158, these boats were the first to operate mid-water pair trawls. In the 1980s *Elizmor* was retired from fishing and converted for use as a pleasure boat. I drew this sketch when I saw her back in Maidens in about 1998.

MANX LILY

Built in 1940 with financial assistance from the Isle of Man government, the *Manx Lily*, PL34, came from John Tyrrell & Sons Ltd of Arklow, along with four other sister boats. However, she was a bit of a tragic boat. In January 1945 she lost two skippers at sea within a week of each other, firstly the acting skipper followed by the official skipper. Then, in 1948, another disaster befell her. On 26 February of that year she was ring-netting with her neighbour boat, *Manx Rose*, PL48, another Tyrrell's boat, off Campbeltown. The fishing was slack that evening and a fleet of ringers anchored in Torrisdale Bay for a few hours to await dawn. A stiff gale blew up quite suddenly and most of the fleet raised anchor and steamed back to Carradale. The crew of the *Manx Lily* didn't and, unknown to her crew, she was swept back onto rocks in appalling visibility and hurricane-force winds. As she hit the shore at Dippen Point the six crew managed to all scramble ashore but the boat was smashed to pieces, a sad end to a lovely boat.

OCEAN PRIDE

Built in 1922 by N.H. Peake & Sons of Newlyn for the Broomfield family, she worked as a mackerel and pilchard drifter. Although rigged as a dipping lugger, she had an auxiliary engine. What makes her different to the normal Cornish lugger is her unusual counter stern which is similar in design to a pre-First World War steam drifter. In the 1930s she was fitted with twin 66hp Kelvin engines which necessitated the engineroom being moved forward where the form was fuller. The foremast was stepped 6ft forward of its original position at the same time. During the Second World War she was requisitioned and by 1950 she had been bought by Ted 'Cuggy' Downing who installed two new 50hp engines about 1962. She was sold again in 1973 to Ian Childs who had crewed aboard her several years before, long-lining and drifting out of St Ives. She was re-engined once again and eventually sold to Les Rowe of Penzance who sails her today, under a full rig, out of the harbour there, although I believe she is again for sale.

GLEN CARRADALE

Built by Walter Reekie of St Monans in 1933 for Lawrence McBride, she had a Kelvin 44hp aboard. In 1941 ownership passed to Alexander Sharp McBride who had a Kelvin 66hp fitted in 1947. She neighboured *Fairy Queen*, CN128, *Nobles Again*, CN37 and *Golden Fleece*, CN170. In 1955 she was sold to Alasdair Gibson of Lochbuie, Mull, and the registration was cancelled in 1962 although she was licenced to carry passengers until 1989. Now I tell you this for a reason, for, whilst doing some field work at Lochaline, I came across her remains on the beach there and wondered what had happened to her. I discovered not a lot, only that she appeared at Lochaline in the late 1980s (probably 1989) and was left alongside the old jetty at the head of the loch. Over ten years she gradually fell apart until the hull collapsed and split into two. When I saw her in 2001 both the stem and sternpost were lying flat, although the hull planking still retained a measure of shape. The rudder and Kelvin stern tube were still there also, the engine having been removed a few years ago. The deck lies atop the beach in two sections. I've a wreck plan drawn at the time if anyone is interested.

HASTINGS BEACH BOAT

In chapter three we mentioned the Hastings beach boats and their elliptical sterns and how the boats working from the beach today – although not many are left – are built on similar lines. Here is one in 2000. The fellow in the foreground is carrying one of the logs they use to run the boats over whilst hauling them away from the water's edge. Most are registered as RX, these port letters standing for 'Rye, port of Sussex'. RE used to be nearby Ramsgate. The boats mostly trawl, trammel- and gill-net in the Channel for sole which is to some extent Marine Stewardship Council accredited, although mackerel and herring from Hastings also has the same accreditation. Unfortunately Hastings boats have been having trouble competing with other boats and the numbers of vessels working off the beach – Britain's only remaining beach-based fishing community of any consequence – and it is feared that before long the whole beach community will collapse and disappear.

MANX CLOVER

Another Isle of Man boat built with financial assistance from the government by Tyrrells in 1941 and registered as PL47 and fished as a drifter/scalloper between 1941 and 1958. Twenty-one-year-old Sheila Kinley's name was picked out of a hat and chosen as the 1st Herring Queen in Peel on 28 August 1952. Sheila was crowned onboard the boat that belonged to her uncle by Lady Cowley who was presented with a model of the boat in a bottle by salesman Mr John Wood from Fife. In 1967 her skipper was Billy McMeiken of Peel, and whilst fishing she fouled her rudder and had to be towed to Peel by the inshore lifeboat. In 1970 she was sold by public auction and purchased by Terry Lang who also bought the *Manx Belle* and the *Manx Rose*. In 1990 she was withdrawn from fishing and purchased by Bill Rothwell in 1992 who converted her for pleasure and moored her at Maryport. Bill eventually moved her to the Isle of Man and sold her for a pound. She was sold again and again until no one was quite sure who owned her. Being in a poor state the Isle of Man government had her broken up in Peel harbour in 2006. The *Ros Cait* and *June Rose* had the same fate, unfortunately quite a common occurrence among boats of that ilk.

BETTY YORKE

This boat I sketched in Arbroath about ten years ago. At the time I knew her owner. She was built in 1938 by Macduff Engineering Co. and first registered as BF434, and was owned out of Macduff for a period in the 1960s/70s. After seeing her in Arbroath I'm pretty sure she was sold although I'm not sure to whom or where. I've since heard that she, too, was broken up because the new owner tried to fix her up but, with bucketfuls of money needing to be spent on her, he got nowhere.

SMILING MORN

Smiling Morn, TT50, is a J. & G. Forbes-built ring-net boat from 1933, typical of the time, varnished above the waterline and beautiful looking with a small pillbox wheelhouse. However, she had been fitted with a 55hp Atlantic engine that gave a lot of trouble throughout the four years she was in Tarbert. Thus she was sold to Wick in 1937 and there she seine-netted under the registration WK70. During the war she was fitted with a machine gun and patrolled out of Wick and Scrabster. She even ferried Winston Churchill at Scapa Flow. After the war she went to Orkney, registered as K827. In 1982 she went south and was bought by her present owner David Merifield who took her to his boatyard on the Medway and now keeps her in tiptop condition for pleasure use.

SUMMER MORN

The 59ft *Summer Morn*, B78, was launched in June 1957 by Alex Noble of Girvan for the Cully family, Portavogie. In her early days she worked the drift- and ring-net for herring and regularly landed into the Isle of

Man. She last fished for herring in 1989, but by then, like the rest of the herring fleet, she was using a trawl. She was then rigged for scallop dredging and worked out of Aberdeen. She was decommissioned soon after taking up dredging and was scrapped as part of the 'legalised vandalism' towards Britain's fishing fleets and its heritage.

LOTHIAN QUEEN

Built as *Lothian Queen*, LH168, by William Weatherhead of Cockenzie in 1936, she fished with a ring-net out of Peel, neighbouring with *Providence*, LH160. One interesting aspect of this boat is the record of the butcher's provisions during a two month period in 1938. The butcher, Dale's of Peel, supplied meat to the value of £4 3s 2d. The following year, again during the summer herring, her meat bill was £4 18s 2d for a three month period. Had meat gone down in price? What was normal was for the boats' account to be settled the following year. During the war this boat was, like many others, requisitioned for war services although quite often there remains a degree of secrecy as to what these boats were up to. After the war she went to Ireland drift-netting and ring-netting. In 1953 she returned back to the east coast of Scotland and was renamed *Ocean Queen*, KY172, working out of Pittenweem. From there she went to Musselburgh, registered as KH415. Over the next twenty years she became registered as BM177 and LO131 before being de-registered in 1985 and converted for pleasure. She's currently based out of Ardrossan and has her original name back.

SCOTTISH MFV

The Scottish MFV is a generic term and the boats are renowned throughout Europe as safe and seaworthy fishing boats, developed first for herring drifting and adopted by the Admiralty as a pattern for boats built during the Second World War for patrol and minesweeping operations. The idea was that after the war they could be passed on to the fishing fleets. There's no doubt that they were fine vessels built by a variety of builders throughout Scotland, each builder having his on particular individual way of shaping the boat. Basically they were all the same – strong bow with sheer, a cruiser stern, and ranging between 45 and 75ft in general. Most had the accommodation aft in coffin bunks with a central table (most ring-netters had this forward), the engineroom forward of that and the fish hold in front of the engineroom, forward bulkhead and sometimes a net room up front. The wheelhouse was aft, again each being the signature of the builder. Some English and Irish yards built similar designs, many of the latter funded by the BIM (Irish Sea Fisheries) and built by Tyrrells as well as yards at Baltimore, Dingle and Killibegs. They were strongly built of larch on oak, double-framed with a small spacing. During the war, some were built less strongly because of the shortage of timber and the rush to get them out. Nevertheless they have stood the test of time as many are still fishing, even if they've been significantly altered, had engine changes and new, roomier wheelhouses and even shelter decks added. Many have been taken out of fishing and converted for pleasure whilst there are still some around the country that have been rammed up the riverbank and turned into houseboats, never to go to sea again. Some have even ventured as far as New Zealand and Australia.

EIGHT

A FEW FISHING BOATS
OF TODAY

INTRODUCTION

Below are a few fishing boats that I've come across recently although you will note that, in the case of some of them, I haven't much to say, believing those to be both destructive and non-selective in the catching abilities and pretty ugly at that. Nevertheless, although the large modern boats have become fairly consistent in design, built from steel and very powerful, it has to be said that conditions for the fishermen onboard have been greatly improved. However, fishing remains a dangerous occupation and it is sometimes quite amazing how these new breed of boats still manage to get into trouble at sea and even lost with all hands. Some think that they are less stable than their older wooden-hulled counterparts, largely due to the full-length shelter deck which must raise the centre of gravity. Having said that, they are still being built as the older boats are replaced. The problem for the industry is that, while they catch more fish, they employ less people. For the fishermen that cannot bode well for the future. As in the farming sector, fishing is being squeezed into fewer hands with more clout. Technology, in the long run, ain't doing it any favours!

GREEK TRAWLER

We captured this Greek trawler on film whilst laying a purse-net within quarter of a mile of the shore in the Euboea Gulf on the East Coast of Greece. Although this was supposedly illegal so close to the shore, there was

no one around to police such actions. However, having said that, the boats themselves are beautifully crafted. In the south of the country I visited a boatyard in 2001 where they were building two of these 80ft boats side by side. Wooden boatbuilding is thriving in Greece, as in many parts of the Mediterranean, and the designs have remained true to their roots.

AUDACIOUS II

Built in 1996 in Spain, this 27.6m trawler with a full-length shelter deck has a 930hp Alpha motor and refrigerated hold. She was first registered as BF83 although her name was changed the same year to *Endurance III* and registered as BF98. Funnily enough, I drew this boat for an article entitled 'Will our children shed a tear when this is decommissioned?' That says it all!

GRP INSHORE BOAT

With the decline in the fortunes of the inshore sector, modern GRP boats have the advantage of needing less maintenance and can be operated by one man. This Cornish boat works a trawl but has two crew.

MODERN BOAT

This boat I saw at Macduff and had to sketch it simply because it was so ugly. It's amazing it floats!

BEAM TRAWLER

This is one of the beam trawlers, belonging to W. Stevenson & Sons, on the slipway at Newlyn. *Twilight II*, PZ137, was built in Holland in 1969 and worked there before coming to Cornwall. At launch she was *Deo Volente*, KW11, and subsequently *Hanny*, HD41. She was still working from Newlyn when I sketched her in 2005. However, there have recently been concerns over the beam trawling fleet and calls for their decommissioning.

DAYSTAR

I once spent three or four days on this boat out of Fraserburgh pair-trawling off Shetland for herring. The boat was massive with refrigerated seawater tanks for keeping the herring fresh. However, after one particular haul in which some ten tons of herring were caught, the skipper decided it wasn't worth turning the pumps on to bring the fish aboard so it was let loose. Being a bit of a conservationist, I was really shocked and depressed about this. It seemed both such a waste of natural resources and an unnecessary pollution because presumably most of the fish would be close to dead and wouldn't survive, probably with burst swim-bladders. Although I can understand the financial side of the operation, it seemed to me that that was what fishing had become. A balance of cost versus time without any concern of the environmental damage. No wonder fishing has such a bad public face in some quarters. When the crew got the net in a mess and had to steam into Lerwick, I left the boat, preferring to get the ferry back to Aberdeen!

JACINTA

Jacinta is a stern trawler once belonging to the well-known Fleetwood trawler owners J. Marr & Sons. Built in 1972, she's older than she might appear. At 50m with a 1,900hp Ruston-Paxman diesel, she's a pretty huge monster that worked the North Atlantic fishing grounds from Greenland to Russia. She holds several records such as the top-earning British trawler (1986 and 1994), and British single landing record at Hull for a twenty-one-day trip (1991). Once withdrawn from service in the mid-1990s she was sold to the Jacinta

Charitable Trust for £1 and since has been opened as a museum where visitors can learn all about the fishing in those northern waters. Docked mostly at Fleetwood, she does sometimes take to the sea, appearing, for example, at the International Festival of the Sea in Portsmouth in 2005. Okay, so she's not a fishing boat of today but she could well be, given her looks!

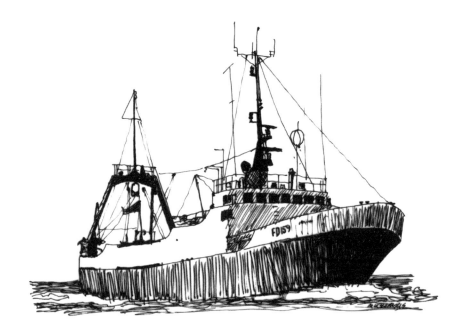

NINE

CONCLUSIONS

Europe has a diverse collection of fishing boats of all types, and most are not only working machines but works of art, put together by men with skills gleaned over many years, learnt from others with even more years' experience. The fishermen themselves learn the same way, keeping traditions that have been passed down through generations, father to son. Ashore a whole host of industries have contributed – sail-making, engineering, timber felling, rope-making, net-making, fish filleting, electricians, metal workers – the list is endless. Fishing continues at a frantic pace, with fewer boats chasing smaller shoals, although landings seem to go up. Industrial trawlers sweeping clean species that mankind will not eat, so that they end up being processed. Stocks of herring and mackerel being processed for their oils, to be sold as supplements, the residue mash being fed to farmed salmon and even the Danish bacon pigs. Stocks are being taken to the brink by international super-trawlers which have been known to plough through the coastal native fishers in their traditional craft, drowning the occupants. Around the coasts, especially the north, new boats are being brought into the industry whilst the older, less efficient ones are being decommissioned, sold off and scrapped. We've seen a few of the fishing boats still working. Now let's have a final glimpse at those that didn't make it.

SUBSIDISED HOUSING

In parts of the country old boats have often been turned upside down and used as roofs, sometimes placed on stone walls, for centuries. On the island of Lindisfarne, Northumberland, a grant has recently helped in the purchasing and positioning of one such boat after the previous one was damaged by vandals. These huts were used as workshops and sheds by fishermen and

their boats would only be inverted once they were beyond their working lifespan, and they would normally be covered in tar or, latterly, felt. I once saw a garage in Shetland roofed in this way and often thought I wouldn't mind living in such a structure!

IMPROVING THE ENVIRONMENT

I sketched this for a tongue-in-cheek postcard of what happens to decommissioned boats. However, in reality, there are dozens of roundabouts and entrances to villages and towns around Europe where these boats have been placed to rot away. Theirs is surely going to be a short lifespan. I remember one particular politician saying that this sort of thing was saving fishing boats for posterity which he thought was a valid reason for them escaping the chopping up process. In many places I've seen similar boats chopped in half down the centre line and used as a serving bar in pubs and restaurants, including one traditional wooden catamaran in a nightclub in Sri Lanka. It's not only Europeans that believe these things make good backdrops.

WATCHFUL ASHORE

The *Watchful* was built in 1959 by Weatherhead & Blackie of Port Seton and first registered as BA124. Her owner was Matt Sloan of Maidens who formed, with his brother Billy aboard the *Wistaria*, a successful – indeed legendary – partnership at the ring-net. Matt came ashore in 1971 and sold the boat the following year to John Morrison of Scalpay and she was renamed *Majestic*, SY137. She was sold again in 1983 to Denis Meenan of Campbeltown who renamed her *Stella Maris*, CN158. She was decommissioned in 1995 and escaped being chopped up, thanks to the effort of Andy Alexander of Maidens who crewed aboard her during her years in Ayrshire and who later became a skipper-owner. She was taken ashore and restored by Kyle and Carrick District Council and placed, as a walk-round exhibit, on the harbour front in Ayr. Although hundreds of boats have been decommissioned throughout Europe and most have been scrapped, a few have escaped this unnecessary government requirement, largely thanks to people like Andy and associations such as the 40+ Fishing Boat Association. Amongst those that have escaped the injustice are the two Cornish luggers *Lindy Lou*, now in Falmouth, and *Happy Return*, restored and maintained by the Mounts Bay Lugger Association of Penzance, the Weatherhead-built *Lively Hope*, BK91, a ring-netter working from St Abbs which was donated to the Scottish Fisheries Museum on decommissioning, *Confide*, PZ741, which is on display at Land's End and the Lowestoft line boat *Annabelle*, LT308, which was taken off into Norfolk to be 'moored' ashore.

BOAT BEING CHOPPED UP

Finally, most don't escape the breakers and numerous boats of historical interest have been destroyed by fire, chainsaw and JCB. This one here was the *Try Again* which I watched being ripped apart by a JCB in Newlyn several years ago. It was hard work for the two blokes doing it; the jib-end of the machine was jab-jabbing away at the deck, having only a slight effect on the hardened timbers. The digger was jumping up and down in its spirited attack upon the boat, the concrete slipway reverberating louder than the object it was trying to turn into matchwood. After a while, splinters of wood and blue flakes of paint fell away onto the concrete below. Eventually a hole appeared which enabled the pointed stabber to delve deeper into the very belly of the boat. Bit by bit, piece by piece, structural parts fell to earth. Once this pile had grown from more than a few jagged scraps into a sizeable heap, the drone of the digger ceased and work proceeded on moving the pile to a skip where it would later be burnt. A sacrifice to the God of civil servants, no doubt; or Mammon! Then the pecking arm started up again and the peck-peck-pecking recommenced with a repeat of the earthy splintering sounds more akin to falling trees than fishing boats. The concrete grumbled under further pressure. So sad and so pointless. Yet I couldn't pull myself away from the action, so absorbed was I by the reality and frustration of it all. For a country proud of its maritime heritage it really is an unjust disgrace that this has been allowed to happen to some of the best fishing boats in the world. However, with policy stemming from Brussels, Britain is not alone. The following is an extract from an article by Vicco Meyer, translated from the German by Hans-Christian Rieck:

> There is a feeling of sadness about the empty basin of the fishing port of Grenaa/Denmark. The plaster of the wheat storage houses is cracking; the old crane is rusting away. Inside the electric case on the pier there is just a mass of disconnected cables. The water is dotted with puddles of fuel. Beside the fishery pier fourteen wooden fishing boats are swaying gently on the water. Ripped-out beauties, the masts cut off, the wheelhouses removed and the engines torn out. Beautiful lines, mighty stems, strong gunwale and elegant canoe-stern. Painted in that soft azure blue that is so typically Danish like the 'Danebrog' (the Danish flag) in front of the houses. Out of the open hulls emerges that special smell of salt, fish, tar, fuel, and wood. For the removal of the engines the decks where cut open and now the engine room and the aft cabin are open to the observer. Strong ribs, 30-40cm apart. The wood of the cut-through beams is still strong and sound. The gunwale, the deck and the planks as wheel show hardly the age of the vessels.

Soon these boats too would follow others to the scrapyard. No recycling here, just an obscene waste of resources, the result of the ill-thought-out policies of a large beurocracy.

INDEX OF TYPES

Herring: A History of the Silver Darlings

MIKE SMYLIE

The story of herring is entwined in the history of commercial fishing. For over two millenia, herring has been commercially caught and its importance to the coastal people of Britiain cannot be measured. At one point tens of thousands were involved in the catching, processing and sale of herring. Mike Smylie looks at the effects of the herring on the people who caught them, the unique way of life, the superstition of the fisher folk, their boats and the communities who lived for the silver darlings.

ISBN 978 0 7524 2988 5   £9.99

The Slopemasts: A History of the Lochfyne Skiffs

MIKE SMYLIE

Although neither extraordinary in design nor pioneering in boat technology, the Lochfyne skiff was the last evolutionary stage in the era of sailing boats in the Clyde area, prior to the advent of motorisation in the first decades of the twentieth century. Furthermore, the design was unique in that it was developed specifically for a different mode of fishing: that was the ring-net that came into use around Tarbert in the 1830s and which was an aggressive way of fishing that, within a century, became generally accepted by Scottish fishermen.

ISBN 978 0 7524 4774 2   £12.99

Working the Welsh Coast

MIKE SMYLIE

The people of Wales, surrounded on three sides by water, have always looked to the sea, and the sea has always played a vital role in the developement of Welsh culture and industry. This well researched and illustrated book looks at the types of vessels used along the coast for both fishing and coastal trade, from Tenby luggers, Mumbles oyster skiffs, Aberporth herring boats, nobbies and coracles to Welsh topsail schooners. Mike Smylie examines different sectors of the Welsh maritime industry and heritage, all in the narrative of a personal journey along the Welsh Coast from the river Severn to the Dee in 2003.

ISBN 0 7524 3244 1   £17.99

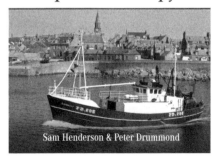

Fishing Boats of Campbeltown Shipyard

SAM HENDERSON

AND PETER DRUMMOND

The boatbuilding industry has always reflected the changing fortunes of the fishing industry. Campbeltown Shipyard diversified its boatbuilding activities in order to survive but competition from foreign yards moved into a new dimension from the mid-nineties onwards. In addition, decommissioning and shrinking quotas have left the Scottish fleet a shadow of its former self. However, by the middle of the first decade of the twenty-first century, things were beginning to look up for the remaining vessels, including several survivors of the boats built by Campbeltown Shipyard.

ISBN 978 0 7524 4765 0   £14.99

Kindly Folks and Bonny Boats

GLORIA WILSON

The boats and fishing communities of Scotland and North-East England from the 1950s to the present, making use of Gloria Wilson's unique collection of photographs. From attractive Scottish wooden-hulled craft to recent steel boats, this book offers a glimpse into a glorious bygone age. Including information on boat design and construction as well as some rarely seen naval architects' line plans, this beautiful book considers the work being done to balance fish conservation with profitable fishing, a pressing issue for the fishing industry of the twenty-first century, and for Britain as a whole.

ISBN 978 0 7524 4907 4   £12.99

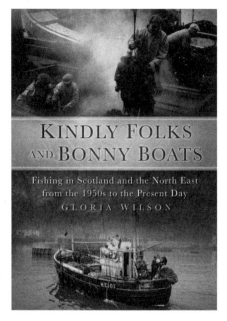

Maritime Wales

JOHN RICHARDS

For centuries the lives of Welsh men and women have been bound up with the sea, as a source of food, employment and communications. All along the coast a variety of shipping places developed, ranging in size from small fishing harbours up to the huge coal ports of south Wales. This well-illustrated book concentrates on the history of ports and harbours in Wales: their periods of growth and decline; the kinds of cargo handled; vessels, owners and builders; and the typical voyages undertaken by local mariners. It is in invaluable reference for anyone interested in this nation's maritime history.

ISBN 978 0 7524 4224 2   £18.99

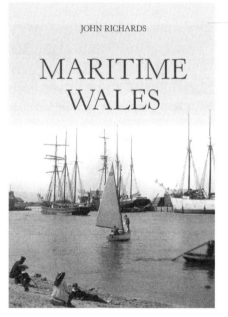

Visit our website and discover thousands of other History Press books.

www.thehistorypress.co.uk

The History Press